Frantic Leadership

How to Grow Leaders, Inspire Others
and Achieve Results

Or

Develop Management potential by
applying new mindset, thinking, and
skills necessary for success.

Christian Hasselberg

Out of the Box Books
Tucson, Arizona

This publication contains the opinions, ideas, and personal experiences of its author. It is sold with the understanding that neither the author nor the publisher is engaged in rendering legal, tax, investment, insurance, financial, accounting, or other professional advice or services. If the reader requires such advice or services, a competent professional should be consulted. Relevant laws vary from state to state. The strategies outlined in this book may not be suitable for every individual and are not guaranteed or warranted to produce any particular results. No warranty is made with respect to the accuracy or completeness of the information contained herein, and both the author and the publisher specifically disclaim any responsibility for any liability, loss, or risk, personal or otherwise, which is incurred as a consequence, directly or indirectly, of the use and application of any of the contents of this book.

ISBN: 978-0-9801855-8-4

Library of Congress Control Number:
2016912483

For information on other books by Christian Hasselberg
visit the publisher's website at:
www.outoftheboxbooks.com

When it comes to books… think Out of the Box!

Out of the Box Books
P.O. Box 64878, Tucson, AZ 85728

For Michelle, Nathan, Victoria, and Karsten
I am blessed to have a great family. Michelle, thank you for your servant's heart and lifetime partnership. You put up with my endless dreaming and projects. I am grateful for your kindness and your love. To my kids, in the words of my friend Bob Zachmeier, "Develop the confidence to set aggressive goals, the discipline to achieve them, and the desire to share your blessings with others." You are the next generation. Make us proud.

For Michael and Susan Train
You are great parents who endured many hardships, loved us all and expected great things from us. Pop, thank you for your military service and teaching me so much at a young age. Mom, you are the best. Thank you for everything.

For Dwight Michael and Susan Rentler
Uncle Mike, you are the closest example of unconditional love that I have witnessed on earth. You love me no matter what. That means so much and sets a fine example. Tia Sue, you are a wonderful helper and such a blessing. Keep Treasure Hunting!

For Dr. Larry and Nancy Alves
I could not have asked for a more interesting and adventurous in-law or, as I say it, out-law experience. Nancy has an amazing heart. While we lost the Doc two years ago, he lives in our hearts.

Table of Contents

TABLE OF CONTENTS

TABLE OF CONTENTS

ACKNOWLEDGEMENTS

Tom Bruenn -- for being a GREAT math teacher, treating me like a son and opening my mind.

Nathan Lancaster -- Idaho firefighter and college roommate who taught me to stay calm under fire (no pun intended).

Lieutenant Colonel Nathan Huntington -- a man's man, Marine Corps helicopter pilot, faithful, and a great friend.

Captain Larry Stein, US Navy, who taught me how to lead by example. I would follow you anywhere.

Robert and Camille Zachmeier, owners of Win3 Realty, a top real estate company in Tucson, AZ. Author of several books, including Sold on Change and A Daily Difference. Bob taught me how truly intuitive people think. I also learned that failure is a path to success. Camille took a chance on me by giving me my first job after the Navy.

Jonathan Green - gave me great support as a developing Integrated Product Team Leader and trusted friend.

Hamilton Garcia -- a great supporter and driven to succeed.

Marlene Thompkins for giving me a shot in the Leadership Development Program. She once told me that I would paint the rose on the rose colored glasses if I had to. Talk about support. For her openness about her own flaws. Always a winner.

ACKNOWLEDGEMENTS

The Arbinger Institute -- For their deep passion to help organizations and families achieve breakthrough results. Their three flagship books, Leadership and Self-Deception, Anatomy of Peace and The Outward Mindset are cornerstones of my leadership philosophy. In the words of Steven R. Covey, I could not recommend them more highly. I would mention them all by name, although that's just not their style.

Darryl Seering aka "Sheldon" -- For rarely saying no to my endless ideas. We shaped the team together.

Richard Beekman aka "E.F. Hutton"-- For your friendship and willingness to bounce ideas. A certified Genius, he would never tell you about it. He once told me that he joined Mensa but quit, saying that it was just a bunch of smart people talking about things that they knew nothing about. He writes math books and studies French for fun. He learns so quickly! He recently wrote a great math book that explains the art of solving complex mathematical problems. Plus, anyone that describes me as iconoclastic (I had to look it up) must be interesting. Stay tuned for more adventures with Uncle Rich and me.

Finally, thank you to my awesome editors, especially my sister Katherine Despres. Also, Richard Beekman, Carla Milligan, Mike Rentler, and Michelle Hasselberg! You helped make the book better, and I am very grateful!

INTRODUCTION

This is not a guru book. My friend Richard Beekman told me that most leadership guru books only need to be about five pages long. His theory is that there is one "great idea," and the author makes an entire book out of it. I want to introduce many ideas for your consideration that is comprehensive leadership wisdom instead of the latest leadership trends.

Whether you are a future leader, developing leader, or an experienced leader, I hope you will find valuable insights that will help you on your life journey. I am grateful for the leaders and biographers who took the time to write books so that I had similar wisdom to apply. I truly hope that you enjoy this book!

It means a lot to me that you would take your valuable time and entrust me with some of it. I hope to educate and entertain. I don't have all of the answers, and I do not claim to be a leadership expert, although some people have called me that. I have also been called lots of other things in my lifetime: **Frantic (my call-sign in the Navy and part of the book title)**, chucklehead, Mud (given to me by my mother), numb nuts, the machine (for my work ethic) and "the smart kid with no common sense" have all made the cut. What other people label you is not important. It is extremely important that you recognize your value as equal to everyone else -- no better and no worse.

This book is broken into three parts. Part one is leadership development for individuals. I call it "Emerging Leadership." Part two is "Applying Leadership." Part three addresses several advanced leadership topics and provides some tips to get you there. I don't claim to have all the answers. You will have to wrestle with these things yourself! Good luck and best wishes! We need more great leaders, who can see the truth amidst clutter and noise. Be courageous and take action!

Part I
Emerging Leadership

1

What is a Leader?

"One of the most important leadership lessons I learned was that oftentimes I was a problem for others and didn't realize it." – Christian Hasselberg (adapted from Arbinger principles)

We were a one-car and two-worker family growing up. That meant hours each week in the car with my brother and sister in the back seat and lots of patience. This was before the days of IPads, IPods, DVD players, or even Sony Walkman's. We had to TALK to each other or use our imagination. As a kid, I did a lot of listening, because that's what kids did. I remember this one time when I was about eight years old; we were picking up my father at his job as K-Mart resident manager in Waterbury, CT, and I was laughing my tail off:

> Pop: "Sheldon is transferring to another store. "
> Mom: "When is he leaving?"
> Pop: "In two or three weeks."
> Mom: "When is the going away party?"
> Pop: "In three or four weeks."

So you think you want to be a leader. I bet Sheldon thought he was a good leader, but obviously he was less than his own hype based on his peers and followers.

One measure of leadership is the business results achieve. Another is what everyone says about you. If you achieve one without the other, your position will be short-lived. And that's when it hits me – sometimes I think like Sheldon and am just as blind.

I'll bet that many of you are leaders already. You might be a team captain, class leader, manager, older sibling, or just about anything. That is great. Lead where you are, and don't worry about gaining additional power. It will come. Believe me, when you are a good leader, people come to you asking for your help.

I have many friends that are very content NOT to be the leader. They don't want the headaches, the hassles, and the extra work involved in "dealing with people." There is nothing wrong with wanting to be a good follower. In fact, it is a prerequisite of leadership. For me, I always found leading people to be the most rewarding part, despite the occasional challenge. Also, if you learn to lead well, then you will deal with less headaches and hassles in the first place.

My thinking about being a leader has changed from the beginning. I used to think that being a leader meant that I had to be better than everyone else – the smartest person in the room. I would use my superior abilities to lead people in the way we should go, kind of like General Patton or Admiral Hyman Rickover. They would follow me because I was smarter, faster and more experienced. I think about King Julius in the movie, Madagascar: "Feel free to bask in my glow!"

I didn't think it particularly mattered if I actually cared about people. Sure, I would give it lip service and tell people what they wanted to hear as a young man, but it rang hollow for me, and it probably rang hollow for them too. I was a hard-worker, and I was pretty self-absorbed but pretending that I wasn't.

I was worried about everything. That worry drove me to work really hard to prove myself, but not necessarily on the right things. Although I was not huge on self-promotion, what people at the top thought of me mattered a lot, and I needed to hear it to feel secure.

In general, *Leadership* **is about defining a vision, influencing people to follow the vision (putting the challenge out there), and taking personal responsibility to serve and encourage collaboration.** *Management,* **on the other hand, is the process of organizing, shepherding and instructing a group to move from one place to another.**

Leadership and management are different but interrelated skills. Some great leaders are also great managers. Some people are good managers but poor leaders. Some people are good leaders but average managers. This topic is confusing because leadership and management, as terms, are often used synonymously.

In my opinion, we, as a society, are pretty good at teaching management behaviors. When I got my Masters in Business Administration (MBA), nearly all of the classes were focused on developing management skills. Accounting, finance, marketing, statistics, project management, operations and organizational behavior are mostly about management development. That is not to say that what we learned was all correct, but at least it was the prevailing wisdom at the time. At the time, ethics in business was not a focus topic. In fact, one of my Ivy League educated instructors, who liked to give me a hard time for being an engineer, got called out for inflating a resume and padding expense accounts. In light of recent scandals, MBA courses now include more ethics in hopes of developing more honorable people.

CHAPTER 1 – WHAT IS A LEADER?

Management and leadership are evolving subjects much like the study of medicine or science. There is much to be learned about both topics, much of what is already discovered but not yet widely accepted in the business and political community.

There are some wonderful books on leadership, many of which I will recommend to you the Appendix. I like to read biographies of interesting people, especially leaders. They offer incredible insightful nuggets that you can apply almost immediately. My favorite book about leadership, called "Leadership and Self-Deception" by the Arbinger Institute, has NOTHING to do with leadership and EVERYTHING to do with leadership at the same time. Every once in a while in life, you will be presented with contradictions like this. Once you really understand what they wrote, you will get it. Once you get it, you will be forever changed. It made a real difference for me and is a constant wrestling match at the same time.

To lead is to serve. Do you really believe that? I used to think leading was about being in charge, barking orders, being the boss, smarter than, better than, entitled to more, etc. This was modeled by many managers I worked for when I was younger. Many leaders lead this way. Some are very smart, capable, powerful people who have become very successful in their careers. So here appears to be another paradox. If abusive people can be successful leaders, why can't I simply do that too? The answer is: You can! The reality is that we are all flawed in some way. I also guarantee you that the abusive leader had some other strength that was highly valued, like expertise in engineering, strong vision (Steve Jobs) or nuclear physics (e.g., Hyman G. Rickover). We can forgive experts who can be abusive at times because we need them. I would also contend that they would have been even **more** effective if they had developed other important leadership skills.

One thing to keep in mind is that it is not right to label people "abusers," "liars," "convicts," etc. In fact, <u>any labeling of others</u> is red flag of a leadership failure in <u>me</u>. Think about that the next time you evaluate a presidential candidate! Would you like to be labeled for the worst thing you have ever done? One of my best friends served prison time. It does not define him.

Are leaders born or made? This is an interesting, age-old question. Some people seem to have natural charisma or something so that people just want to be around them, even from an early age. Other kids are shy and are eager to fit in, so they follow. The question is: Can leadership be taught? The answer of course is: Yes. The point is to start where you are, and to remember it is never too late to learn more. I can tell you from experience that every place I have ever worked has invested a great deal of time and money to develop their leaders and managers. Some training programs were more effective than others, but the common theme is that leadership is a skill that can be developed and improved upon.

Throughout the book, I will share with stories from my life or my friend's lives that illustrate a topic. They might be either work-related or not, since leadership occurs where you are, and you take it with you everywhere.

CHAPTER 1 – WHAT IS A LEADER?

So what is your goal and your vision to improve your leadership acumen?

FRANTIC LEADERSHIP

2

Leadership Disciplines

"…plans are useless, but planning is indispensable." Dwight D Eisenhower

"Customers will never love a company unless the employees love it first." Simon Sinek

Simply put, **strategy is creating the plan, and tactics are making the plan work.** It is a little bit more complex than that, but the mnemonic is a simple enough description. At the strategic level, a good leader develops Mission, Vision, Objectives, and Goals (which start developing into tactics).

Mission – Why we exist and how we help our customers in one sentence. It forces you to articulate the mission in a way that everyone can know and keeps it simple. It also sharpens your focus so that you can evaluate all of your activities against your mission statement. You also want to be careful not to make your mission statement too broad. Keep it focused on what you actually do. A good mission statement will inspire and inform an organization. Then the team will know what is acceptable and what is out of bounds. Here are some examples. Think about them and whether you really understand what they do.

- "Dedication to the highest quality of Customer Service delivered with a sense of warmth, friendliness, individual pride, and Company Spirit." – Southwest Airlines
- "Improve the living conditions for low-income families in Chester County, PA. We transform substandard houses into warmer, safer, and drier homes; and despair into hope." – Good Works (shameless plug for my friend Bob Beggs)
- "To organize the world's information and make it universally accessible and useful." – Google

- "To maintain, train and equip combat-ready naval forces capable of winning wars, deterring aggression and maintaining freedom of the seas." – US Navy
- "We change mindset." – Arbinger Institute
- "Saving people money so they can live better." – Walmart
- "To provide our clients the best possible service available and to provide superior collection results." – ICS Collection Agency

Do you see how most of these mission statements are outward facing? <u>Say what you do from the customer's point of view and make it inspiring.</u>

Vision – What we want to become or achieve. It is the to-be state, an inspirational aspiration. Here are some examples:

- "To be earth's most customer-centric company; to build a place where people can come to find and discover anything they might want to buy online." -- Amazon
- "Create a better everyday life for people" – IKEA
- "A safe and healthy home for every person." – Rebuilding Together St. Louis
- "To provide a free world-class education to anyone anywhere." – Khan Academy
- "To make people happy." -- Disney

Objectives – High-level statements of intent that define what we will do to achieve the vision. These often get confused with goals. These are higher level, such as an objective to achieve a level of customer satisfaction, quality, or innovation. Here are some examples:

- Develop the next generation software.
- Invent a cure for cancer.
- Double the business.
- Acquire companies that complement our adjacencies.
- Outsource excess work.
- Expand into other markets.
- Achieve profit margin of 15%.
- Divest all but our core businesses.
- Be #1 or #2 in all of our markets.

Goals – Specific, measurable (preferably) statements that break the objectives into actionable time-constrained chunks.

The prevailing wisdom is that goals should be SMART (Specific, Measurable, Achievable, Realistic, and Time-constrained). If someone says, "I want to lose weight," this is certainly an excellent goal, but it's far too vague. It would be better to say something like. I want to lose 10 pounds in 10 weeks. Do you see the difference?

One thing you will get hanging out with me is to question the prevailing wisdom (iconoclastic). Sometimes SMART goals make a lot of sense. Other times, it is a pain in the neck and not worth the trouble. (There is a good book called "How to Measure Anything" by Donald Hubbard if this interests you.) If you end up measuring the wrong things because they are easy to measure, you can encourage the wrong behaviors, frustrate everyone and cause great harm. For example, how would you measure a team with a perfect safety record to be "safer?" Maybe you could measure how many times we talked about safety or how many times we took a preventive measure or how many times we walked around and looked for safe behaviors. At the end of the day, it is hard to improve upon perfect, so what did you really accomplish? In my mind, safety is a spectrum from unsafe to safe, and there is a cost/benefit study to evaluate the value of making oneself safer. I could live in a bubble and accomplish nothing but be very safe. After a while, the team simply gets sick of safety and the meaningless measurements. That's the last thing you want!

Oftentimes organizations will also share their values. Values are incredibly important. If you re-read some of the mission and vision statements, some of them creatively have values built into them. At the same time, any need to document my values questions whether I actually value them. It is a way of trying to align everyone to a common set of values and principles when things have gone sideways. My team has a set of operating principles. Once I think that everyone has got it, they will go into the trash.

What are your long-term objectives? These are things you want to accomplish over several years. Once you've set the long-term objectives, establish short-term goals; monthly, weekly and daily actions that will move you toward the long-term objectives. After your goals are established, they need to be communicated to others who can help you achieve them. Also, make them visible within the organization. Share them with anyone who can help you achieve them. Measure your progress.

Tactics – The way to go about implementing the goals.

One question that comes up is how much time should a leader spend on the strategy vs. day-to-day tactics? The answer to the strategic vs. tactical question depends on the responsibilities of the leader. Some jobs are more tactical in nature, and some are more strategic. I have found that most jobs require a combination of both, and failure to focus on one of them creates all sorts of risks, issues or missed opportunities. In a first line leader position, the mix might be 20% strategic and 80% tactical. As the leader becomes more senior, the leader must shift how he/she spends time.

I am going to change gears a little bit and talk about the discipline of obtaining, processing and using information. Information is moving faster than ever, and a leader can be quickly overwhelmed by the flood of e-mails, phone calls, meetings, etc. and lose sight of the big picture.

The lifeline of leadership is information. Your job as a leader is to find ways to get the right information quickly, analyze it, and act. The corollary job is to know what information is not needed. We are bombarded with information, much of which is noise, garbage and half-truths. When I was in the Navy, we had a system called "all source intelligence," meaning that we obtained our data from various sources, some of them highly classified. Our job was to turn data into fused information. A large percentage of information was from news sources like CNN. They also have a network of people keeping watch around the world. There are different kinds of information, and I will provide examples of them below.

When I was in the Intelligence community, I would spend many nights and weekends keeping watch. While most of America is sleeping, there is a small group of dedicated professionals paying close attention to keep us safe and trying to predict and prevent the next major incident. I had one boss who insisted that we call our fellow commands every shift looking for "the scoop." The truth was that we all had the same information, so most of these calls were not required. But we did them because we were ordered to do so. After a while, you could tell that the other commands were getting tired of our calls. We were getting a reputation as a bunch of idiots, all because the boss created this work. I don't say this to bash the boss but to ask, have I ever created needless work? And I regret to say yes. So, learn what is most important.

Managing Information:

Tactical information is that which is important to know as soon as possible. Tactical information has a short shelf-life. It is valuable for immediate situational awareness, and its value declines rapidly over time. Here are some examples:

- The tank battalion is moving south.
- The stock just hit 23.
- There was a flasher on Main St.
- Shaq is sitting at Harvard Square.

It is quite possible that some information is almost completely useless to all but a very select few individuals. Most of what is in my Facebook news feed is useless, but I wade through it looking for nuggets. Other examples include a picture of my dead cat, scientific theories that only two people in the world can understand, and twitter posts that gossip about the latest celebrity.

Strategic information is knowledge, like long-term plans and big picture thinking. The higher you move up in leadership, the more strategic you must become. There are whole books just on strategic thinking. It is important; failure in strategy can destroy a game-changing opportunity.

CHAPTER 2 – LEADERSHIP DISCIPLINES

Determining someone else's strategy can be determined by piecing together a lot of small pieces of data into a coherent picture or plan. Examples include US foreign policy, a company's decision to invest in a new market, or a specific technology. Strategic information lasts a long time and has a longer shelf-life. Its value is good for long-term planning and declines very slowly over time.

Frantic Sidebar – Technology Shifts

A few years back, an IT department was approached about upgrading to the new iPhones and Androids instead of the Blackberries. The IT team asked questions, which were more like statements, like, "what do you need that for! Everything that you can do on the IPad, you can do on the Blackberry. You can email, you can check your calendar. You can surf the web. You don't need an iPhone." So the people went away frustrated. What is interesting was that everything they said was true. (Of course the real obstacle is money. Who wants to spring for more equipment when it is not in the budget?) If you were to ask them what they use at home, I would guess that 100% of them they would say an Android and iPhone. Why not use a Blackberry? After all, you just said you can do everything you need on them! (By the way, the Blackberry Z10 improved the experience considerably.)

The reason why everyone shifted when iPhone came out was because it was a game changing experience in the human machine interface. Everybody knows it. You have to think about the short-term and long-term impacts of game changing technology shifts.

Some information is good in certain instances but otherwise has little value. I call this **reference information**: things that are nice to know when I need it but otherwise has very little usefulness. Examples include my Hilton Honors number, my friend's street address, the number of US Presidents, the combination to a lock, or a boss's birthday.

I found that my brain may have trouble retrieving reference information readily. However, if someone prompts me or gives me a hint, my brain will know it to be true absolutely. Some people are wonderful at retrieving information from their brains. That is a special type of intelligence or excellent training. Thankfully, the cloud has helped solve this problem.

Here I will make a plug for Evernote or a similar cloud storage company. I really like the ability to tag and store all sort of notes and artifacts. The tagging makes it easier to retrieve later. It even does handwriting recognition. Pretty cool.

Here is an interesting question: How should we store different kinds of information as leaders? Do we store it all the same?

3

Continuous Learning and Development

"The greater the island of knowledge, the greater the shoreline of ignorance." Garth Rosell, Socrates, Plato and a few other smart guys.

We live in an era where there lifelong learning is the new normal. A friend of mine said that his Computer Science department at Washington University had on the wall that everything you learn here will be obsolete in three years. Yikes! In software, that was very accurate then. Now, it is accurate in almost every field, as computers and technology infiltrate every aspect of society. Data analytics is a game changer. Farmers can improve their output without having to buy more land. Baseball players can improve their on-base percentage. (See my recommendation about reading Moneyball.) Teachers can share real-time information with students across the world.

I love to learn. I get interested in topics and pursue them vigorously. I develop a level of proficiency and then move on. While I rarely become an expert, I seem to have become good at a lot of things, which has given me a perspective of looking at challenges from several experiential viewpoints. So I am more of a generalist. We also need people who become experts in specialized fields.

I also like to read about interesting people. There are many amazing people in the world from which we can learn and are very inspirational!

It is very important to invest in yourself to stay relevant. I think about it like this -- The company you work for is doing what it can (we hope) to find work for people and provide value to customers. You must be prepared to perform that work. If you are not, then you will be left behind. The days of loyalty are long gone. You must continually add new value. You can complain about it or embrace it. As I told my kids, "If kindergarten is kicking your butt, I've got bad news about the rest of your life" (This was quoted from the book, Sh#t my Dad Says, which was hilarious). You have to keep learning.

In the era of corporate cutbacks, personal development has become more the responsibility of the individual. There are great ways to get education though. Many organizations have tuition assistance programs that are great and encourage learning.

Think about where the company is going or what next level you are looking to achieve in your life. That might mean getting an advanced degree, taking a course, or finding a mentor. It could also be volunteering for additional duties at work that stretch your skills. It could be as simple as watching a YouTube video. I can fix almost anything around the house with curiosity and the help of Google, YouTube and a set of tools.

Many people want more money and a promotion. I hear that all of the time. What I tell them is to demonstrate the characteristics and skills of that advanced position now. What behaviors and experiences are needed for the new position? Which do you have, and which do you need to develop? Build a personal development plan. If you take a mentality of waiting for the promotion to demonstrate those skills, then you will lose. There is someone else smarter and hungrier who will beat you.

Many companies have leadership training programs. Some of them are pretty well thought-out and meaningful, while others are little more than a communication medium for the latest corporate buzzwords. Some classes are so basic that you have to wonder if anyone got anything out of them. I would submit that if seasoned leaders are getting a lot of value out of these basic level classes, then they really need to shake up the leadership. Perhaps something else is broken.

Do you have a mentor – or three mentors? This can be a great relationship where a senior person takes an interest in you and your career. You also share with them personal experiences of what life is like where you work. They appreciate the perspective as well. Good mentor/mentee relationships are open and honest. You have to be open to correction. If the mentor says you need to change, try not to get defensive. Instead, take an honest look about the possible truth in the statement. Take the truth and act, and throw away the rest.

The bottom line is that you have to own both your career and your continuing education. The days of waiting for things to happen and going with the flow are over. If you are not learning and growing, then you are falling behind. It is easier than ever for a company to outsource jobs for lower cost structures. Therefore, your job is to become more valuable to your employer or the industry every day. That comes from and with education, wisdom and experience.

4

Leadership and Power

"Power corrupts. Absolute power corrupts absolutely."– John Dalberg-Acton

There is a strong relationship between leadership and power, more specifically how leaders acquire power. A softer term for power is influence, which I prefer. When I was a midshipman in the Navy ROTC, the instructor taught me that a leader develops power in several ways. Quite frankly, since I am taking this from memory from twenty years ago, it is likely that I am missing one or two items in this model and adapting it as well. But you'll get the idea.

Legitimate Power -- The instructor held his collar containing his officer rank and said, "This is my legitimate power. I outrank you. While that may be enough power for me to get you to do something, this power won't last long if it is not backed up by other means, like respect." In other words, positional power only goes so far.

Another aspect of legitimate power / influence is how successful you can be whether the people on your team work directly for you or not. It is easier to lead people who have to do what they are told or else. I know of some leaders who insist that being in control of everyone is the only way things will work properly. For some leaders, that may be true. I think you should aspire to be better than that, however.

While I may have legitimate power, I try not to lean on it. Instead, work hard to earn trust and develop other forms of power within the team. One way to avoid relying on legitimate power too much is to lead a volunteer organization. Since there is almost nothing stopping volunteers from quitting, you have to learn to lead people without having a lot of legitimate power. People will stay because they believe in the mission and vision and because they are treated well. After all, this is their personal time. How would you want to be treated on your personal time?

Expert Power -- This is influence obtained as a result of developing a skill. Since you have that skill, people will listen to you.

What skills are you developing where you can become the expert? My friend Rich thinks that if you can commit between 5,000-10,000 hours of time to something, you can become an expert. That's probably about right. Think about the things that you've put that much time into. Make a list. For example, mine would be (in no particular order):

- Leadership
- Teaching
- Changing mindset in others
- Software engineering
- Database administration
- Test data management systems
- Aircraft health management systems
- Systems thinking
- Military intelligence
- Information technology
- The Bible
- Real estate investing
- Project management
- Track and cross country
- Cycling

Then you could make a list of areas where you are growing to become or are not quite an expert. For me, the list would be (this might be the "know enough to be dangerous" list!):

- Harmonica and drums
- Negotiations
- Mediation
- Conflict Transformation
- Foreign languages
- Lean+/six sigma
- Clojure programming
- Data analytics
- Fixing up houses

What's the point? It's useful to know what you are good at and where your real expertise lies. It's also a confidence builder and a decision aid. Organizing people around their expertise and sharing knowledge is one way to grow an organization. It also provides clarity on a biography or a resume.

CHAPTER 4 – LEADERSHIP AND POWER

My father, a helicopter crew chief, told me stories of how his helicopter crews were shot down in Southeast Asia three times. One time, he and the rest of the crew were declared missing in action in the jungle. Although he was not the senior member of the helicopter crew, he knew much more about jungle survival than the pilots thanks to intense military training and my grandfather, who was a World War II sailor and taught my father celestial navigation, small arms and lots of other skills as a boy. The officers agreed that my father (at age 19) would make the decisions to lead them out of the jungle. His first decision was to go in the opposite direction, further into the jungle, from the base where the enemy would expect them to go. 45 days later, they made it back to civilization, much thinner but alive. It was unheard of to be missing in a hostile jungle for that long and survive. At the end of the journey, one of the officers said to him in a moment of excitement, "Son of a gun, you did it!" It also earned him the medal just below the Medal of Honor, the Distinguished Service Cross. (In fact, he has three of them. Welcome home, and thank you for your service Pop!)

Can you imagine what would have happened if the officers started disagreeing with him early on, grumbling and subverting his authority? We're going to go which way??? But that is too far! It would be easier to go that way... He wouldn't have been in my life, or he would have been in a prison camp. This is serious business. Therefore, respect the experts regardless of their title.

Influence Power -- This is a type of power achieved by earning respect and improving one's influence over other people. It is the subject of most of the book. Think about how you want to follow the guy with all of the good ideas. It is the ability to get someone to change, and people, no matter how entrenched, can change in an instant. Showing people a better future and asking them to help achieve it can be very inspiring if it is a worthwhile objective delivered in the right way.

Charismatic Power -- Some people win influence with their charm or passion or personality. I think of people like Martin Luther King Jr., Donald Trump, Barack Obama, Colin Powell, Steve Jobs, Bill Clinton, Elizabeth Dole, or Glenn Beck. (I tried to use the whole political spectrum!)

I believe that this skill can also be developed. Some people are masterful. Think about people you have met that you would just follow anywhere. I have had leaders like that. One of them was Navy officer Larry Stein. He was a fellow junior officer in the Navy with me, a few years senior to me. He took an interest in my career and exemplified hard work and setting high expectations. He knew how to serve his customers and how to build relationships. He was inspiring. I knew that he cared about me, and I wanted to work hard for him in return. He wasn't big on politics or trying to make himself look good. Last time I heard from him, he had earned the rank of Captain, which is a pretty select group in the Intelligence community. If he personally called and asked for my help, I would drop everything and go. Shouldn't we all aspire to earn that kind of loyalty?

Coercive Power -- Some people lord over others by way of negative reinforcement or punishment. In a war zone or intense time-constrained environment, it might be the right thing to do in the moment. Sometimes, there is not time for debate.

This works better in a command and control type environment. Generally, it's not the best way to achieve results over the long term. When I worked at McDonalds as a grill guy, time was of the essence. People wanted their food quickly, as it was part of the experience. The managers could do my job and every other job in the place. Some of them were not kind and threatened to fire us as a way to motivate. It worked for a while. The workers banded together in misery. Eventually, I got tired of the working environment and found a better job. (Side note: I think everyone should have a job like that in order to appreciate other jobs. It puts things in perspective.)

Network Power. This kind of social power comes from being well-connected to others within the organization. People come to this person because they know that you will recommend someone who will help them. I remember one time when I switched jobs and had to rebuild my network. It took a long time to rebuild, and I felt exposed until I had developed my own network again.

I have one person on my team, Carla, who seems to know everybody. She has a vast network of people who help us get things done. One of the cool things about Carla is that she does not care if you are the CEO or the janitor. She will add you to her network. (Besides, sometimes the smartest person in the room is the janitor.) I rely on her network often to help us reach out to a different part of the organization, and she helps me build my network as well.

Gossip or Toxic Power. Some people feel like they have leverage if they keep the information to themselves or stir up the rumor mill, thinking that people will gravitate to those who are in the know or curry favor. There are elements of truth in what they say, along with embellishments. Of course, this kind of perceived power is not helpful to achieving the long-term results we need and is actually counter-productive.

I had one employee who loved to stir up the rumor mill, speculate and generally start trouble for the leadership. It generally gets back to management when someone says, "People are saying that…" Note the passive voice. The first question I ask is, "Which people?" Usually, someone will answer eventually. After a while, we figured out that one particular person was starting these rumors and gossip. We asked him to stop, and he said that we were "taking away his power!" I never thought of gossip and rumor starting as a form of power until he put it that way. He can no longer complain, whine and spread false rumors. It is possible that he perceived, from his point of view, that the rumors were true. I don't know, but it is reasonable to ask a person to do their best at work, and gossip power is not part of "best work" to me.

I know of other workers who purposely start rumors to see who they can trust and who spreads and acts upon the rumors. I am not a big fan of this tactic either, as it seems to hurt one's credibility.

What's your primary influencing style? Can you appreciate the other styles and when they might be useful?

5

What do Good Leaders Do?

"There is a big difference between doing things right and doing the right thing." LT Joey Gardner

There are many behaviors and skills that leaders must do and many more that leaders <u>should</u> do. For example, it is tradition in the military that officers often eat last, or they are the ones serving the food at the barbeque. The idea is not to copy these behaviors but to develop a service mentality and be prepared to do whatever your conscience informs you to do. If you do those things, you will be ok.

Leaders provide a compelling vision of the future. Where do we want to be in five years? How do we get there? One sentence. Be short and sweet. Clarity is important.

Leaders provide challenging work for the team. People want a challenge, so find ways to make work interesting and meaningful for people. Connect the dots to show how each persons' contributions matter to team success. Celebrate success!

Leaders build a collaborative environment. They understand that one person's success is dependent on other's success. Imagine 10 people trying to build a house and each person has their own job. The plumber doesn't care what the electrician or carpenter does. He or she just does the plumbing. Do you think that will hurt the quality of the project? What if he cuts the electrical wires to get his pipes into place? It sounds silly, but that kind of thing happens all of the time. We want the plumber to provide an excellent product and service in a way that enables others to succeed as well.

Leaders hold themselves accountable to the highest standards first. The best leaders do not "hold people accountable"; instead, they create an environment where the team members hold themselves accountable. If that is done well, there will not be a great need to hold anyone accountable, because the job will already be done. In fact, the only thing to hold others accountable for will be the self-accountability that they had agreed upon.

Leaders practice what they preach. For example, you have no moral authority to talk about cost cutting if you fly first class, get preferred parking, a car, and other perks -- while the rest of the team flies coach and watches you. Now, if you NEED these things to do your job, then that is different. But if you don't need them, I recommend you give them up. For example, one leader gave up his parking spot. It is a small example, but if everyone else had to walk a quarter mile to work, what made him special? Prevent opportunities for resentment and entitlement.

Good leaders admit when they are wrong. I have had people coach me and tell me that I should never apologize to the team. I think that is rubbish. If an apology is needed, why not apologize? Would you rather them stew and resent you? Admit when you are wrong. It doesn't make you weak. You actually lose followers by denying the truth. I am sure that this might seem counter-cultural in some work settings. I had one coworker tell me that apologies make me weak. Perhaps, but strength is not my goal. Achieving results is my goal, and I have learned that creating space for people to see me as human is helpful to develop collaboration. Some people are so good, so polished that they seem to never make mistakes. I am striving to be more like them. In the meantime, I will admit when I fail. Besides, failure is simply a pathway to success.

Good leaders ask questions! You will be amazed how many people will fail to ask simple questions for fear of appearing dumb. Once the dumb question is out there, it gives people space to learn, and often I have learned that people are just as clueless as I am. In other words, don't be afraid to look like the dumb one. The dumbest ones are those happy to remain ignorant. And, ignoring issues about which you <u>should</u> know will not help your leadership skills.

CHAPTER 5 – WHAT DO GOOD LEADERS DO?

Early in my Navy career, I was in a review of a new, large computer system to be deployed first on our ship. We were in a big room with my boss, his boss and many mid and senior officers as well as government contractors. The contractors were explaining how the ship should be the launch platform for the upgraded system. This wasn't a navy system any longer. It was a joint system (meaning multiple services use it), the big buzzword at the time. In truth, I doubt it was very joint at all, more likely a necessity; to get funding, you had to claim it to be multi-service. It was supposed to subsume other existing systems into a larger system. Close to closing the deal, the contractors went into great detail that the hardware was ready and that this was low risk. When they were done with the presentation, I asked, "What about the software?" It had not occurred to anyone in the room to give the Navy an assessment of the risks associated with the upgrade of the software. As a Computer Science major in college, that seemed pretty important to me.

I got a lot of strange looks, "Who the heck are you and why are you speaking?" I started to feel intimidated and thought that I better not talk any more. Clearly, the question was not welcome and they were about to ignore it until my boss's boss did something I will never forget. He supported me by saying, "This is Ensign Hasselberg. He works for me and has a Computer Science degree. You will listen to him and answer his question." In terms of supporting me, he could not have done better. I would have done just about anything for CAPT Dave Maresh. How are you being supportive like CAPT Maresh?

37

Good leaders are great encouragers and often act as the Chief Affirmation Officer on the team. If you are the head of encouragement, teach and listen, you earn the right to correct them. When I was on loan to a team recently, I noticed that one particular leader went out of his way each day to say something nice to every person on the team. It might have been a little forced at times, but overall I appreciated the gesture and the effort to build relationships and check in with people.

Remember there is no difference between people and results. Great results are achieved by people. You grow people by asking them to achieve great results. Many leaders get this wrong, and think it is ok or necessary to mistreat people in order to achieve results. This is very short-sighted and will lose people in the long run.

Good leaders have discipline. You will never get to where you are going without it. I have a friend Bob who values every minute of his day. "We only have so much time." He is a great entrepreneur, and the more time he has to think about his business and his customers, the better and more successful he is. He told me one time that he cut out all TV from his life. At the time, I thought he was radical, but ten years later, I get it. He also did an annual assessment about how he balanced his life. He called it the wheel of fortune. He evaluated things like how much he exercised, how much he read, how much he worked, his spiritual life, etc. He then plotted it on a radar chart. If he was low in one area, he would develop a plan to improve. For example, he would get up at 5:00am to write a book or to go running. He would change his diet. He would stick to it too (until he hosted the "put the weight back on" party). That's discipline!

A final thing to think about is how you personally define success as a leader and as a person. In high school I was voted "Most Likely to Succeed" along with Cat and Lisa. I spent many years wrestling with what success meant. I felt like I had to live up to some standard. Back then, we might have thought of success as the person with the most money. I don't think that is it at all. I had one employee who was convinced that when he reached a six figure salary, he had "made it." That was his definition of success. Several years later, I checked in with him when he made it. I asked him if it was satisfying. Not surprisingly, he said no. I told him that perhaps his ladder of success was leaning against the wrong wall. So I sent him to think about success again.

For me, success is to find meaning and satisfaction in my work, to care about others and help them succeed, to live an honorable life, to love God with all my heart, and to touch a tomorrow that I will never see. If I earn a decent wage, that is a bonus! I don't claim to have been always successful, but that is my objective.

Phew! There are a lot of things to think about in this chapter. I hope you take some time and think about how you are leading. What do you think I missed? Send me a note at christian@franticleader.com and I will add the good ones to the web site.

6

Have Faith

"Believe in yourself, the organization, others and a higher power."– Christian Hasselberg

Have faith in what? That's a great question! I cannot answer this for you. I can say with some certainty that you cannot lead without having some faith. Here are some things in which I have faith. I hope some of these resonate with you.

Have faith that the organization supports you. They asked you to help them in whatever leadership capacity that you have. They are grooming you for a better future through training and experience, and you need to get prepared for it. Sometimes, you might not agree with everything. That's ok. Say your piece respectfully, and continue doing your best. I learned a long time ago that life's not fair, but in general, people get what's coming to them.

Have faith in your abilities. You would be amazed at how much does not get done because people don't even bother to try. The negative self-talk stifles them. I know because I have the same problem. You have to fight against it. There are whole industries around motivational speaking and self-help books. They do very well because, among other reasons, people lack confidence. Perhaps someone told you that you were no good or couldn't improve at something growing up. Maybe you had a tough childhood. Some people take that and use it as motivation. Others wallow in the negativity and become self-fulfilling prophecies. Some of the best innovations come from the nay-sayers telling a person that "it can't be done" or "you will never be able to do that." My friend Brandi's high school counselor from a small Illinois town told her that she would never be a lawyer. Today, she is a wife and mother of four great kids. She gives back much of her time to volunteer work. She invests in wonderful friendships. She also is a successful attorney. Enough said!

Some people, myself included, focus more on what is wrong than what is right. It's just how we see the world. We notice what needs to be fixed. That includes when we're analyzing ourselves. That can take us down a negative path, always dwelling on what's wrong and worrying about correcting it. We have to look harder for the good things. They are there; we just don't see them as clearly. I try to hang around with people who see the positive things to balance me out.

Have faith in yourself. OK – here is a pep talk if you are looking for some confidence. You are unique and special. There is no one else like you. You have terrific qualities and skills. You are in situations where nobody else can perform as well as you can. In fact, you were *meant* to do these things. People care about you, too. Sometimes, they may not show it, might not even know how to show it, or show it in ways that you don't understand. But people do care about you. So go thank them. More importantly, go care about them in return.

You have an education and are getting more every day. You worked hard and earned it. You are prepared for the next challenge. If you are not, you have the tools and skills to go prepare for it. You are always capable of learning more.

The sum of your experiences produced wisdom. You don't claim to know it all, and you seek more wisdom. You made some bad decisions and learned from them. They do not define you. You made some good decisions too! Remember them once in a while. You survived the tough times and came out stronger on the other side. You got small wins. Small wins become big wins over time.

Did you do your very best? Why not? Why not do your very best from now on? Excellence can and will be a part of the future you.

Have faith in other people. You don't have to be the smartest person in the room. Learn to embrace others and honor them for what they have to contribute. They are not perfect, but neither are you. Most people want to do their best. Besides, you can't do much of anything in leadership without others, so they are pretty darn important!

Have faith that miracles happen. I wanted to share with you a miracle that I had the privilege in which to be involved. I'll go through the details and let you decide if it was a miracle. I am completely convinced.

I met Terry McCollum at church in 1999. He was the Sunday school teacher for the young married class that Michelle and I attended in Tucson, AZ. He and his wife Nikki volunteered their time to teach us every Sunday for years. I knew him well. He loved God, his family, his friends, people, baseball, singing, and the University of Arizona Wildcats basketball team. If there was such a thing as a #1 fan, Terry would have been in the running as a permanent season ticket holder. Terry mentioned to me once that he had been on the road and watched an Arizona basketball game at every away stadium in the PAC-10 except for the University of Washington and Washington State University.

He would talk about his friends during class. He has one really special best friend from college that he missed dearly named Malcolm. The class reunion was coming, and Terry was so excited to see him. He called Malcolm to find out that he was not feeling well. I think he said that his back hurt and that he could not drive to the reunion. Terry would have none of it. Malcolm needed to be there. Terry volunteered to drive him. Terry said that they would stop every 10 minutes along the side of the road if they had to so that his friend could rest. It was that important to Terry that they be together. After a while, Malcolm agreed to come, and Terry was elated. As the days to the reunion drew near, Terry reflected on the past and looked forward to sharing precious memories with his best friend. Suddenly, Malcom's brother called Terry to tell him that he forbade his brother from going. He was not going, and that's that. Click. Terry was upset. He was fuming underneath the whole time at the reunion. While it was nice to see everyone, he felt like Malcolm's brother robbed him of his joy. Malcolm died a couple of years later, never having seen Terry, and Terry carried this anger against that brother around quietly for years.

One day, it occurred to me to do something nice for Terry to thank him for years of mentoring and friendship. I got the ok from his first wife Nikki (he only had one, and he introduced her as "my first wife"). I made the arrangements and presented him with a flyer telling him that this weekend, we are going to Pullman, Washington to watch the Arizona Wildcats play the Washington State University (WSU) Cougars. The Cougars played the "most boring style of basketball," according to Terry, where they slow the game down by passing the ball around until the shot clock almost expires. The slow-down game strategy often is effective in limiting high-powered offenses like Arizona. Anyway, he was thrilled, and off we went. Since I had gone to college in Moscow, Idaho (very close to Pullman), I knew the area very well. We stayed with Dick and Carol Wilson (the nicest people – shameless plug) and toured the University of Idaho for the day before the evening game. We lucked out because the Lionel Hampton jazz festival was going on, and we got to sit in on some rehearsals. He loved music. We then made the short eight mile trek to Pullman, Washington. I put on my red Arizona t-shirt and got there early. Our seats were not very good, and there were a lot of empty seats around us. It was a thrilling game. It was Feb 24, 2005 and Arizona won in overtime, 57-56.

At one point, I walked down a little closer, and this guy starts talking to me about Tucson. I am polite and tell him I live there. He tells me that he decided to come to the game on a whim. It's a 2-3 hour drive from central Washington where he lived. He hadn't been to a game in years and hadn't been to Tucson in years either. He starts asking me about people I might know, and these people are all long before my time there. So I wave Terry, a lifelong Tucson native, down. They get to talking, and I just listen. They start connecting. They know a lot of the same people. They have a lot in common.

It turns out that this man is Terry's best friend Malcolm's brother! It is the very man whom Terry has harbored bitterness for years for that phone call. They get to talking about Malcolm, and this man gave Terry the rest of the story, that Malcolm was much worse than he described to Terry on the phone. The trip would have killed him. There was no way he could have gone. He was helping to keep his brother alive.

That was exactly what Terry needed to finally release that bitterness and anger that bothered him for years. They exchanged phone numbers and talked a few more times after that.

While we had a great trip, that meeting made the trip magical. It was amazing. Until the day Terry died of cancer, Terry never failed to thank me for taking him on that trip. It was always the first thing we talked about. The pleasure was mine Terry, and I miss you.

Was that a miracle? I think so. Could it have all been just luck? Think about how many things would have had to be just right in order to get two people who lived a thousand miles apart into the same stadium, in the same section, at the same time, find each other and able to connect so that Terry's forgiveness could take place. I have no doubt that God arranged that meeting. You have to decide for yourself. But when I need to have faith in a higher power amidst my trials, I think about Terry's miracle.

So, why is it important to have faith? There are things that we can't control. There are people who will let you down. Bad things happen to good people. Life is not fair. Sometimes, you have to take a risk and stick out your neck. Having faith gives us the confidence to see things through and helps us to do our best in the face of trying circumstances. I wish for you to develop faith and confidence in yourself, others, and God as you progress through your career and, more importantly, your life.

7

Personal Traits of a Leader

"Any need to document my values questions whether I really value them". -- Arbinger Institute

This chapter is about personal traits to develop and maintain as a leader. There may be some overlap from other chapters. That is somewhat by design because it is hard to separate what leaders do from their personal characteristics.

When you join an organization, you will note that the values of the organization may not be the same as society's values. First of all, society's values change over time, and not always for the better. Each organization has its own values, as a subset of the larger society. The values of the organization will ultimately determine its success or failure.

"Any need to document my values questions whether I really value them." (Arbinger Institute) What a thought provoking statement! The truth is that we write down our values as an organization because we are trying to constantly reinforce them in the hearts of everyone on the team. No matter where you are from or what you have done, we can align around these values. But just because we write them down does not mean that people will buy into them.

Here are some values from various organizations around the world:

- Honor, Courage, Commitment – US Navy
- LIFE -- Leadership, Integrity, Flexibility and Efficiency – Bayer
- Charts the Course, Sets High Expectations, Inspires Others, Finds a Way, Lives the Boeing Values, Delivers Results – The Boeing Company Leadership Attributes

- QUALITY, CUSTOMER Satisfaction, LEADERSHIP, INTEGRITY, Value PEOPLE, SUPPLIERS are Team Members – Northrop Grumman

Northrop Grumman likely had an issue with the way they treated suppliers and explicitly put verbiage into their value statement to address it. So, it is likely that they aspire to have these values but have not achieved them totally yet.

Ok – so onto the list of personal traits. There are many, and it is not exhaustive. I welcome your comments.

Integrity. Integrity is one of your most important traits. It is not negotiable. Honesty, respect, fairness and other similar mores need to be your compass. You have to be able to look at yourself in the mirror and sleep at night. Nobody is perfect, and everyone has made mistakes. Take personal responsibility for them, and do what you can to make them right. You are who you are today, in large part, thanks to your previous decisions and responses, both good and bad. Embrace it!

Leaders look for how they were responsible for the problem and fix it. My kids just spilled paint all over the carpet. Apparently, they tried a science experiment to roll a can of paint down the stairs to see what would happen. My seven year old son Nathan came downstairs and said to me, "Dad, you might want to see the stairs." Notice that he did not go to mom -- smart kid! Meanwhile, my five year old daughter was busy hiding the stains with toys and blankets! It looked pretty bad, but I didn't come down too hard on them. I really appreciated Nathan's honesty and had to make a special point of rewarding the excellent behavior. Also, I thought about how many times I passed by that paint can at the top of the stairs and did not move it. I encourage them to be curious. I created the environment. In some way, I was responsible as well.

Leaders are brutally honest with themselves -- not only intellectually but also about where they have been irresponsible. Self-reflection is important for growth and development. If you were screwing up, why wouldn't you want to hear about it?

Leaders listen and create a safe environment. You don't want to be in a situation where people stop bringing you bad news. Don't breed an environment of fear. If so, people won't bring you bad news, and they will cut corners to make themselves look good. They won't tell you what they did wrong. They will make your job harder, because they perceive their job as making themselves look good. They do that by stepping on others or being supremely concerned about how they are seen.

Leaders set a bar <u>above ethics</u> to excellence – a strong moral compass.

I have a real estate broker's license, and I have met many people who have gotten wealthy in real estate. Some of these approaches are trade secrets that people will share with you at seminars for a price. When I attended some of them, I found that what they did was perfectly legal, but it did not meet my criteria of ethics and morals. Therefore, I just couldn't go about it. You have to decide what you are willing to do to make a buck. Personally, I didn't care to get rich by taking advantage of people in distress. There is a fine line between legal and right. When we cloud those things, it puts pressure on the entire financial system. The more people we can develop who can see this difference and do the right thing, the better.

I heard recently from someone that, "everyone lies a little on their resume." Really? I don't. I want to put my best self forward, and I want it to be helpful and informative. I have accomplished much to put on there, as have you. Just because "everyone else is doing it" does not make it right. Stay true to your values.

Leaders are humble – well some of them are. I like to think of myself as a member of the team but in a different role. Every role is important. You see, leadership positions have occupational hazards of self-importance and superiority. For me, I try to avoid that by staying grounded and focusing on getting the job done and thinking deeply about my impact on others.

Leaders are inclusive. Early in my career, I would get frustrated when someone else didn't work as fast or as hard as I did. But the truth is, they are not me. It was an important lesson in diversity. They have different abilities and skills. The results may have taken longer but the quality of work was better than what I would have done in that case. Leadership is a team sport. The sum of the team is greater than any one leader -- most of the time.

Leaders have clarity. That means strategic clarity as well as operational clarity to solve day to day challenges. We run into complex problems that are not in the textbooks. You have to find your way through it.

I was asking a mentor, who is now CEO of a company, how he deals with bad news and stressful days. I was struggling at my level. The problems that he has on any given day are many times worse than mine. He gave me great advice:

1. Come into work expecting problems. That is why you are here. If no problems occurred, it was a good day.
2. Have faith.
3. Live your values through the problem. As much as you want to lash out, live your values. It is during a crisis that people watch you most closely.

Leaders focus on getting things done. The great ones figure out how to make it happen.

Trust your followers. Do not take responsibility away from them. The Navy trusted me to protect an aircraft carrier and maintain situational awareness for 8 hours every day of the six-month deployment. I was one of three people who had that job. I took it very seriously, as over 5,000 lives and billions of dollars were at stake.

Leaders have good judgment.
My pastor told a story of a mentee asking questions of his mentor.

Mentee: How do I get to the top?
Mentor: Experience.
Mentee: How do I gain experience?
Mentor: Good decisions.
Mentee: How do I learn to make good decisions?
Mentor: Bad decisions.

Leaders have a positive outlook. It is catchy. Alternatively, negativity is catchy too. For example, do you find the flaw or find the opportunity? You will see what you look for. Take the extra time when a subordinate needs your help.

Look at it the other way – how would you like to be treated? A leader might say to you, "Get to the point – I haven't got all day!" Will you be as likely to bring them more issues?

Leaders understand and adjust their risk taking tolerance. Generally, successful entrepreneurs understand this well. There is a lot of uncertainty in starting a venture. Many of them fail for all sorts of reasons. You have to have the stomach for leadership.

Leaders are good at finding talent. More on this in Chapter 24.

Leaders create excitement about the future. One person talked about good leaders sustaining an operation. Great leaders accelerate it. (John Maxwell)

Leaders are genuine/authentic. They are genuinely concerned about the welfare of others, being thoughtful and responsible citizens, and making the world a better place. Some so-called "leaders" are sociopaths who are attracted to having power over other people.

Who inspires you? If you wrote a book, who would be on your acknowledgement list? Aspire to be the leader that would want to learn from and follow.

8

Be a Good Follower - Working for Other Leaders

"What we do with the young officers is we give them so many collateral duties that they crack. Then we take one away." -- CAPT Dave Maresh

"Ensigns are like fuses. When one burns out, you just throw him away and replace him with another." – Lieutenant Commander Bill Ullman

That was my introduction to life aboard an aircraft carrier. I was the new ensign, the junior guy. The senior officers would love to pepper me with intelligence trivia questions that I did not know. They were actually disappointed when I got an answer correct. It was all in good fun though. I think it made them feel better that they knew more, but more importantly, it made me realize how little I actually knew and how much work I would have to do in order to excel at being a follower of these officers. I knew that they were mostly kidding with me. I also got the message. I knew what they wanted and what was expected. Results.

In order to be a good follower, you have to study other leaders and observe closely. What are they like? Where do they excel, and where do they struggle? What do they expect you to do? It is up to you to learn those expectations. Don't wait to be told.

Loyalty. Wouldn't you want your people to be loyal to you? Sure. But don't take it to an extreme. You should be loyal to the organization first before the leader, but sometimes that gets out of whack. I remember in my early career one time when something was not done and the senior leader asked me why. Honestly, I explained that my boss hadn't done something yet. He just laughed and said, "Way to bilge your boss Chris. You will go far." I didn't mean to do that; I was just being honest. So you learn – sometimes presenting things in a way that makes others look bad is not very helpful. Perhaps I should have delayed a little and circled back first. Maybe I should have taken more responsibility in the moment even though it was not mine. I don't know. These are some of the issues that you will need to consider.

Advisor. You hope that you earn the right over time to become part of your boss's advisory panel. Present good ideas, be trustworthy and reliable. Part of your job is to ensure that your boss is successful.

Support. I think it was Murphy's Law that said, "Keep your boss's boss off of your boss's back." What results are they trying to achieve? How can I help them achieve those results? You have to know how your boss's boss measures success so that you can help achieve it.

Self-Accountability. When you work for someone else, you owe them accountability for what you have been assigned to do. Rather than wait for them to ask, offer how you are doing voluntarily. Be honest. Don't try to look good. If you work for a good leader, he or she would rather have the truth than a charade. If you work for a bad leader who only wants to hear good news, then it is more challenging. The leader needs to create a safe place for the truth to come out. If it does not, the organization will suffer, and you will probably want to look for another role. If things are not going well, tell the leader what the plan is to do better. Don't just bring bad news; think about how to solve it as well as what plan is in place if the problem recurs.

"Lead, follow, or get out of the way." -- CAPT Larry Stein

Larry Stein took me aside and noticed that I was waffling in my decision-making as a young officer. While it hurt a little, I never forgot the lesson. I am being paid to lead or follow. Pick one. I also realized that I would serve the team better by following Larry rather than trying to one-up him. He had more experience and I had a lot to learn from him.

Think about strong leaders in your past or present. What did you learn from them, and what did you notice about their character as a follower?

9

The Leadership Secret: Caring

"There is a distinct difference between caring and looking like you care" -- Unknown

I have read many books that claim to have the THE SECRET to leadership success. If we do this one thing well, then we will be successful! After all, it worked for me! Surely it will work for you, right? Phooey.

Being an engineer, I am a big root cause guy. In medicine, for example, we can address the symptoms or we can address the root cause. I get poison ivy pretty easily, and most of the treatments deal with the symptoms. If you don't get the urushiol (oily organic allergen) off of your skin, you are hosed, and the rash will get worse.

The idea is often the same with leadership (and many people) problems. I have found that most of the books address the symptoms (our behaviors). Others take a crack at talking about esoteric things like culture or attitude. But what if there is a root cause that we can actually teach and understand, puts a common language around it and addresses the root cause in a way that will make many of the symptoms go away? Well, it's not a myth, and it's one of the greatest discoveries of the 20th century.

A man named C. Terry Warner and the Arbinger Institute have figured this out in Philosophy and have created a language, models and frameworks that are incredibly helpful. They have several books (Leadership and Self-Deception, Anatomy of Peace, and The Outward Mindset) and facilitate for organizations large and small around the world. This is life-changing stuff, folks. It provides incredible clarity and has the potential to change the world. I would strongly encourage you to check these books out.

Arbinger talks about the idea that I am the problem and do not know it and am resisting the idea that I am the problem. I am not going to try to teach this to you, as they are much better trained to do so. But think about it this way – wouldn't you rather work for someone who cared about you as a person? If you work for someone who doesn't care about you, what does that feel like? Are you as likely to do your best?

So I aspire to be a leader who cares about others. How do you learn to care? I remember one person asking it like this: Are you trying to be a better leader or a better person? I think the answer is YES. In order to be a better leader, I must also be a better person. Being a better person has immense benefits in all aspects of life. In fact, I had one colleague tell me how it saved his marriage.

Think about leaders that cared about you. What did they do and how did they show it? Leaders that cared about me and took an interest in my development. They were open and relationship oriented. They thought about my needs and offered to help. They encouraged me. They understood that my success was their success and behaved accordingly. They let me try new things. They asked for and wanted my opinion. They were patient.

You have to learn to care about (dare I say love) people. There is no substitute for caring, and people will see through the fakes and phonies. They may still do their best, but it will be in spite of you. They will care more about themselves and making sure that they look good than in the mission of the organization. Let's just hope that those two objectives do not compete, which they often will.

I have to ask myself this question often: if I really cared, what might I do differently? Upon considering the question, I often found out that I didn't care as much as I thought I did. It's a humbling admission, although it's also something that I have the power to fix. Then go do one of those things. You might be amazed at the impact you will have.

Some organizations teach leadership that is focused on policy adherence and ensuring proper behaviors. A person who cares about others will likely stand apart in such an environment because the person has more character and integrity. Failing to address the root causes and addressing only the symptoms is not working. This is the systemic flaw in most leadership development programs.

Learning to be more caring takes time and practice. In some sense, I spent many years thinking incorrectly, and it will take time to unpack some of that baggage and move forward. Don't be too hard on yourself. Just keep trying.

Look to other people who care well. What do they do and why? Why did that idea occur to them? Do you think about others? Are you curious? Can you be more patient? Are you a good listener? Practice. Believe it or not, it is actually far more efficient to care than to not care. Trust me.

CHAPTER 9 – THE LEADERSHIP SECRET: CARING

Here are Steven Blackwood's seven ways to make the world a better place. These seem relevant and practical:

1) Pay it forward - don't let fear stop you
2) Commit a random act of kindness today - every day
3) Never underestimate the power of encouragement
4) Be sensitive to those around you
5) Look for opportunities to do little things for people
6) Dare to be different
7) Be the change you wish to see in this world

Steven and Cindi Blackwood
www.alexblackwoodfoundation.org.

10

Question Conventional Wisdom

"Why shouldn't we reinvent the wheel?" Christian Hasselberg

On my first midshipman cruise aboard the USS Bainbridge, some of the junior officers said that I looked like Hyman Rickover, who was the father of the nuclear navy and probably one of the most important men of the 20th Century. I think that was what got me interested in learning more about him. So I bought his biography many years ago. He went against the grain very often (iconoclastic). If you ever met him, you would never forget. Many people talk about how what a positive influence he had on them, even though he rarely affirmed, and was actually quite mean at times. He had tremendous expert power in engineering, education, discipline and was very well read. Some people say he was the greatest engineer ever.

Best Practices

This chapter is about questioning the conventional wisdom. I find that many teams and groups get into ruts where they rely on processes instead of brain power. Someone declares that the "process" is the best practice. Then the process gets documented. From there, everyone is expected to follow it – one size fits all. If the process does not work or is too complex, you might be able to tailor it, but that comes at a cost. In some cases, the cost is defensiveness about the need for the process as-is and an arduous journey not worth fighting about why you need a waiver. After all, if every team needed a waiver, then one would have to admit that the process is onerous or flawed. You have to balance process with the value that it brings to a customer and not have processes for its own sake. After a while, nobody even owns the process anymore. It is just there. That's one example of why we have to question conventional wisdom.

Sometimes, the right things to do are opposite from what many leadership gurus advise. Why is that? It's is not that they are wrong; it is that they don't necessarily understand the true root causes of their success and failures. Therefore, the solutions that they recommend do not always work the next time around. Also, as I discussed in chapter 9, if your mindset is in the direction of others, it is possible to actually do and say the *wrong* things and still pull off success! Similarly, if your mindset is inward, even the right behaviors can backfire.

For example, Management by Walking Around (MBWA) was a great recommendation several years ago. Basically, it was a message to get out of your office and see what is happening in the workforce. In general, it does make good sense to be informed about what is happening and to talk to people. However, what if you have great micro-management tendencies? You tell others what to do and over-manage them. Do you think that walking around will be helpful? People will get tired of you checking up on them. It will actually make things worse. What about a scenario where you think everyone else is inferior to you? If you look down on everyone, they will see you walking around as patronizing. In fact, people will notice that things work better when you are on vacation! "You can't talk your way out of a problem you behaved your way into." (Steven R. Covey)

The Watchful Manager

Let's say that I suspect that certain people on the team are not pulling their weight. Perhaps I suspect that they are talking too much about non-work-related things or spending too much time on the internet. So I might start looking for examples of this behavior and start collecting a list of all the times that they talked too much or surfed too much. That certainly seems appropriate. But is it in all cases? **When I get laser-focused on what others are doing wrong and start to see them in ways that get me angry and upset, I almost automatically stop noticing what they are doing right!** All I notice are the bad things. The confrontation that occurs has me with a laundry list of their faults for them to fix. But is it a balanced list? Am I really as laser focused on efficiency as I claim to be? Worse, when I show up with this list and fail to mention a single thing that they are doing right (or give token treatment), how do you think they will react?

I have had some leaders who were convinced that their method of leadership is the most effective and that everyone should do things the way they did. If the person has enough power, he or she can direct large organizations to change approaches. Sometimes, this is a great approach, but it often has its problems. First, what happens if the solution to their challenge is not the same as the leader's challenge? It won't solve the problem! Second, what if another approach would work better? The cost of implementing would be higher than needed. Also, the leader is making an assumption that all problems in the organization will be solved with this approach, which is highly suspect. Finally, sometimes nobody really understands the problems in the trenches anyway.

Think about the problem carefully. Oftentimes, leaders don't really understand the problem in the first place. There are lots of ways to help us understand the problems and get to the root causes of the problems. Some are more complex than others. It is important to be able to frame the problem properly. I call that the problem narrative. One of them I like is cause and effect thinking, using 5-why analysis and other root cause methods. By the way, when I am not caring about others, my framing of the problem is likely skewed, and I limit the possible solutions.

Best Tool for the Job

Let's say that I have a splinter in my finger, and I would like to fix the problem. I can use tweezers and Vaseline, or I can use a saw to amputate my arm. Either way, the splinter problem is solved. Which way seems to make more sense though? Another way of thinking about it is using a hammer when a screw driver would be more effective. A good leader has many tools at his or her disposal.

We have to be careful that our leadership approaches do not tell people how to solve the problems. Instead, empower the team to solve the problem in the best way that they know. It is usually better to achieve a team agreement in the path to follow.

My friend Rich Beekman told me a story about asking a group of people how to weigh a giraffe with a common bathroom scale. The adults were pretty perplexed about how to do it. The children, however, figured it out very quickly. Chainsaw the giraffe, and weigh the parts. Aren't children wonderful?

I have a friend, Paul Winters, whose company recently had a "Hack-a-thon" week, where everyone was empowered, for a week, to work together to build whatever they wanted -- something cool and (hopefully) helpful to the workplace. It is very engaging and encourages everyone to bring innovative solutions. I loved this idea.

"**Don't reinvent the wheel**." Why not? The wheel has been reinvented many times for many purposes. Can you imagine all of us trying to use a caveman wheel for everything that we do? That's ridiculous. Obviously, if there is a suitable wheel that meets my requirements, then there is no sense inventing a new one, but that goes back to systems thinking and matching needs with solutions.

I used an example earlier about the iPhone and the Blackberry. By that reasoning, why would Steve Jobs have bothered to reinvent the smart phone when Blackberry had already done it? The iPhone is one of the most successful products in history. The human machine interface was so much better. My 3 year old can use an iPhone with ease, and he can't even read.

Taking Responsibility for your Emotions

Here's one that needs attention. "You made me mad." Another one I hear is road rage – "The other drivers made me mad." Really? Am I really responsible for your emotions? You'd like to think that I am, but it is not the full truth. If you are mad, it is because you chose to get mad. (You may have made that choice long ago, but that is the topic of another book). Think about agency. As a real estate broker, I have an agency relationship with a client. The client allows me to represent them in the transaction. Similarly, in the "you made me mad" scenario, *you gave me agency to push your buttons.*

At the end of the day, I can only provoke; you have to choose to get angry (or envious or bitter or impatient). How do I know? Two reasons:

1. I could do the same thing to two people, and one will get mad, and the other will say, "He's just having a bad day."

2. Consider the alternative. We are all slaves to other people, and at any given moment, someone else has the power to change my emotions. That seems ludicrous.

As much as I want to blame others for my impatience, my anger, and other blaming emotions, a strong leader must realize and confront the truth – that I am responsible for many of my negative emotions. Am I responsible for all of them? I am not sure – but certainly many of them.

If you are offended, you took it. Someone didn't give it to you. Learn to look for the truth in what someone is saying. Then throw the rest away. Don't take it personally.

What conventional wisdom do you need to question? What is bothering you about the assumptions with which you are living? Get out there and challenge the wisdom. Develop your own.

Part II
Applying
Leadership

11

Developing Leadership Skills

"Don't worry about whether they are listening to you. Worry that they are watching you all of the time."
– Anonymous

I have attended many leadership development programs over the years and have invested thousands of hours studying leadership. One thing I have learned is: Just because it was published by some prestigious school does not mean that it is good advice.

In my experience, I have found that this foundational work by the Center for Effective Organizations (University of Southern California) (CEO – how clever) is a very solid read. It is called "Using Experience to Develop Managerial Talent. A Professional's Guide to On-the-Job Development" written by Morgan McCall, Esther Hutchinson and Virginia Homes from 1989. I found it their web site here:
http://ceo.usc.edu/pdf/g89_8.pdf

Awesome! Anyway, the paper talks about how leaders develop, and what kinds of assignments help grow people. The paper broke down seven different kinds of assignments:
Early jobs –
Non-manager work experience
First time supervising people
Short-term assignments
Line to Staff switch (corporate staff roles)
Project/Task Force – temporary assignments alone or as a team
Major Development Assignments
Starting from scratch
Fix-it/Turn-it-around
Increases in scope, people, dollars, and functions to manage

CHAPTER 11 – DEVELOPING LEADERSHIP SKILLS

The paper examines the importance of exposure to "significant people," such as role models or superiors with exceptional (good or bad) attributes. They also reference the importance of watching "values playing out" and giving snapshots of behavior that demonstrate values.

Another development opportunity is taking advantage of circumstances, such as a subordinate performance problem, business failures and mistakes, personal traumas, or breaking a rut.

As I tell my kids all of the time: "Life's not fair!" Sometimes drastic measures will be taken, and we must learn from demotions, missed promotions, lousy jobs, or getting exiled. Sometimes, it can be very lonely, but you must stick to your values.

Finally, there are opportunities away from work to learn and grow, such as coursework, volunteering, or other purely personal experiences.

I am really glad that this old publication is still available. I don't want to spoil it for you. It's a great read and will give you much to think about. For example, instead of concentrating on the next big career move, maybe you can volunteer for a short-term assignment to gain some valuable skills while in the job that you have!

Leadership is something developed both by doing it and by watching others do it. I like this quote from a retired senior leader: "Leaders take risks, they are innovative, they make creative choices…they reach out to help others succeed." As we discussed earlier, it is not about power – it is about a personal vision, communicating that vision clearly, engaging a team so that "we" can get there, and inspiring others to get there.

If this kind of thinking gets you all fired up, then you have the potential to be a great leader! ☺

12

Fixing a Struggling Project

"Hope is not a leadership best practice." -- Anonymous

I was on one program where things were not going well. The program had multiple, small contracts that would bridge us to the next contract. The time it took to execute a contract was, for example, about six months. But the short-term contract was only for three months. Before long, we were in what I call a contracting "death spiral." If something was not in scope for this contract, we needed to add it to the next contract. After a while we had many contracts in work at the same time. We had existing contracts, proposals, contract extensions, bridge contracts, contract lapses (where we had to reassign people) and lots of delays. The delays were partially caused because the people who were supposed to do the work were constantly working on the next contract proposal and did not have time to actually perform the work on the existing contract! How do you fix something like this?

In another example, sometimes our desire to close the deal forces us to sign up for work that is not achievable in the time, budget and expectations that were agreed upon. For example, if the organization has to close a big deal in order to reach an orders goal (or some other arbitrary deadline) by the end of the year, then that puts pressure on the person to accept worse terms. Sometimes we call it taking a "challenge" in order to close the deal. The challenge will ultimately end up manifesting itself into an earnings challenge, because the company has a high probability to get less earnings or even lose money on the deal.

To make matters worse, the project often gets passed to the next manager, who is stuck with the problems and gets blamed for failing to execute the program. Some leaders seem to have a short memory when it comes to the past and instead emphasizes the need for the leader to find a way and be more innovative. The decisions made early in a project often drive the most cost downstream. Worse, the contract documents are either not clear or promised too much.

I have a co-worker, Ted, whom I respect and from whom I have learned much. He said to me recently when dealing with a challenge that anything is possible as long as it is not "illegal, immoral, unethical or defies the laws of physics." That creative thinking mentality is what is needed in tough times.

In one example of a "challenge" that I accepted, in order for us to achieve our goals, I had to ask my team to work many unpaid nights and weekends in order to meet our customer's expectations. In other words, I accepted a bad deal, and then the entire team suffered. At the time, it was the best deal I thought I could get, but it was still a tough lesson to learn. Thankfully, it was a relatively small project, and we got through it in a few months. Sometimes these projects are huge with large-scale impacts, and I have watched teams suffer for years.

Nobody likes surprises. Do your best to keep people informed.

Meetings. One common problem is that meetings get out of control for many reasons. Sometimes, there are too many people in working meetings to be effective. Other times, the objectives and outcomes are unclear. Also, nobody takes notes.

Then there is the hijacker who tries to change the subject. You have to figure this stuff out and keep the team focused. There are some funny Tripp and Tyler videos on YouTube that talk about meetings satirically. Check them out!

Take responsibility for your mistakes. I used to attend a church where I was nominated to be on the Finance Team, along with a few of my friends. One in particular was Cindy. She had a degree in accounting, and I had recently finished my MBA. We were excited to help and serve. She was a shark with the financial statement. In terms of scope and scale, the church budget was $500k per year. We were surprised to see that the church had a balloon payment mortgage due in three years and even more surprised that the church trustees had not approved the deal. There was little budget discipline, little accountability, no finance policy manual, no savings plan, and high optimism for incoming offerings. We had our work cut out for us! Over a period of two years, we addressed each of these issues, with a lot of prayer, which would become a basis for better decision making and financial management for years to come. During the second year, I was the finance chairman, something that will matter a lot in a minute.

One day during the second year, the Pastor read a note to the congregation during the first service that he resigned -- immediately. He just walked out. We sat there in the chairs stunned! He then proceeded to recruit church members in the parking lot for a new church that he planned to start. The other pastors, deacons, other leaders and I gathered in his old office in light of the crisis. I had no idea what was going on. Slowly, the personnel team and the deacons began spilling the beans about what was happening behind the scenes, but it was still the "fog of war." That's an expression I use to describe the beginning of an event when all the facts are not yet known. Apparently, there were serious issues of leadership, working together and accountability that the deacons were working to improve.

They looked at me and said, "You are the Finance Chairman. You are in charge." I was pretty sure that I was not next in the church succession plan! Surely, the associate pastor or the head of the deacons would get this blessing. I got the impression very quickly that everyone else in the room looked spent and dejected, even the other pastors. So I stepped up to the plate. In hindsight, I'm really glad I did because it was the beginning of a rebuilding opportunity, and I was in on the ground floor.

My first jobs were to pick up the outgoing Pastor's computer at his house and determine his severance package. Unfortunately, he did not merit a severance package since he did not put in proper notice. There were some who wanted to press the point, and I felt that it was the wrong thing to do to withhold it. **Trust your gut and do the right thing even if he may not have deserved it**. I also thought it might show our goodwill to upset church members. Surprisingly, nobody wanted to go with me to his house! He and I had always gotten along, so I wasn't too concerned about a confrontation.

It was an awkward meeting. I asked him how he was doing which was a main concern for me. He thanked me for allowing him to keep his severance. He wanted to keep his computer, but I drew the line there because I knew he was recruiting members, and I didn't want him using church property to attempt to sabotage the church. We found a compromise that was acceptable. I felt sorry for him; he looked really tired and upset. I really didn't harbor any ill will toward him. We just had to move forward.

The next day, the church secretary called me at my work place right before lunch and asked me if she should cut off his e-mail address. It sounded like a no-brainer to me until she said that he comingled church business in his personal e-mail. I told her to keep it active for a little while to see what church business there was. I thought about it over lunch, and it was nagging me. So I called her back after lunch and told her to cut it off. If someone needs us, they can call the church office. **Trust your gut and do the right thing.** Well, it was about one e-mail too late. An angry church member sent the Pastor a personal note, and the secretary sent back a short reply. Crap.

I didn't know the person very well, and I sensed that I should call him and apologize, which I did that evening. I never took such an ass-chewing in my life. He told me how I always had it in for the pastor, that I was arrogant, and a whole bunch of other choice words. He was angry, and I was to blame. While 90% of what he said was not true, I just took it. He needed to vent. But he was right about one thing, I made the wrong call with the e-mail, if only for an hour, and I regretted it.

CHAPTER 12 – FIXING A STRUGGLING PROJECT

You learn your mettle when you are falsely accused. How you respond in the face of false accusations says a lot about your character. I took it too personally.

After a little while one of the other pastors, a great guy, stepped up and assumed the admin duties, which made sense since he was there day to day, and I had a full time job. I was relieved of duty! In short order, we got an interim pastor named Mitch. Mitch had worked this roundup before and was used to this kind of situation. He asked all the right questions as well as any General I had ever met. Where do the trustees stand? How many people have left? How are the finances? One by one, he asked if we were committed to seeing this through. We were. **In a crisis, cut the bull and focus on what matters.**

It was ugly for a few months, and it got worse before it got better. Finances were tight. We lost a lot of members who did not know what actually happened. There were significant HR problems that had occurred, and you just can't talk about them. People felt hurt and confused, and we had to tighten the belt. I was pretty glad that we had set up a savings/rainy day fund eighteen months ago.

Looking back, I would not want go through that again, but I will say that it was a great learning experience. I now know what to do through experiential development, by watching great leaders, and learning from other examples.

13

Develop a Common Language

"Get everyone on the same page first." -- Unknown

Developing a common way of communicating is important for organizations. It is hard enough to get work done. It gets even harder if people are not on the same page. Was that 3 feet or 3 meters? What does C.O.P. stand for? Why did the BCWP (Budgeted Cost of the Work Performed) stay constant when the ACWP (Actual Cost of the Work Performed) grew by 100 hours? What does Health Management mean? You get the idea.

Watch your words. There is an old military joke about "Securing a Building." If you told the Army to secure the building, they would occupy and defend it. If you told the Marines to secure the building, they would storm it. If you told the Navy to secure the building, they would turn out the lights and lock the door. If you told the Air Force to secure the building, they would obtain a six month lease with an option to buy!

Acronyms are tough too. In every organization, there is jargon and acronyms to make life easier. Until you learn the acronyms, you are at a disadvantage. Try to be patient with the new people and avoid excessive acronym usage with people who do not understand. One organization tried to collect every acronym in the company, and published a book. It was over 1,000 pages. If you looked up PRF, you might have 15 different choices! Talk about complexity! Try to keep things simple for people.

Language is a big deal. My friend Rich Beekman once told me we should stop calling a traffic incident an "accident" and use "mishap" because of the difference in connotation. An accident just happens. A mishap is preventable. The Navy has this figured out. They have a regular summary of mishaps. We can study mishaps to prevent the conditions that led to them. We can learn from them.

Is there a good language for this skill we call leadership? Maybe. Many gurus, psychologists, and others have invented models to explain leadership qualities, some of which I reference here. These models help frame the discussion like a metaphor (I know – I used a simile).

Metaphors and labels can be dangerous, and they frame people's thinking. They tend to oversimplify complex issues. As a leader, you need to carefully monitor how your team uses metaphors to describe issues. People use metaphors because others do not have the time or desire to learn the details, so it is easier to use a metaphor the person might understand.

There is a good likelihood that the metaphor does not match the situation very well. It can also evoke an emotional response to the uninitiated. I catch myself doing this often. Take the 2012 budget issues we had in the U.S. government. We used the term "fiscal cliff" to describe it. What does that mean to you? It sounds pretty bad, like the economy is racing down the Grand Canyon. Boom! Crash! Dogs and Cats living together...mass carnage. Here is another recent example: Our nation has a credit limit. We are spending far more than we are generating in revenue. We call our credit limit "the debt ceiling," which of course needs to be raised in order for the government to keep borrowing more money. It must be nice that we can legislate an increase to our credit limit. I would like to try that with my bank sometime. Generally, when I reach the ceiling, I have to take things out of the house in order to make room for more. But the government is just "raising the roof."

Here is another example: Some people describe Social Security as an entitlement program. Others describe it as a "Ponzi Scheme." Both of those labels create emotional images in our heads. My uncle reminded me recently that he paid his money into Social Security for 45 years, and he wants his money back. He believes that calling it an entitlement program is an insult to hardworking Americans and companies who paid into the program. Like it or not, the words in the original legislation describe the benefit as: " Every qualified individual ... shall be *entitled* to receive, with respect to the period beginning on the date he attains the age of sixty-five..." In other words, the word "entitlement" obviously has different meanings. In the long run, we will be better off just stating facts and data, choosing our words carefully to avoid confusion. It is a development skill to master.

In the work setting, we have overloaded terms that mean different things to different people. A leader must take the time to ensure that the team is speaking the same language. Sometimes a leader has to enforce the issue, but in the right way. I am sure that I annoy my family when I try to correct their language at the wrong time. So know when it is most helpful to correct people. Pick your battles.

Here are some possibly misleading metaphors to consider I've heard in the past few weeks:
- Tip of the iceberg

- Sucking chest wound
- A quart low
- 4th and long
- Bottom of the ninth with two out
- In the 11th hour
- Terrible problem
- The sky is falling
- Brings the system to its knees
- Another disastrous result
- Broken
- Ugly girlfriend
- Overly dramatic

You don't need to editorialize like this. Sometimes, these expressions take on a life of their own and cause all kinds of additional work because that is all that gets remembered.

Finally, let me introduce you to a concept called fat vs. thin language. Fat language full of ambiguity and lacks specifics. Thin language is very clear and specific. Our job as leaders is to "lean out" the language to figure out or explain exactly what is happening. Learn to ask questions that will evoke thin language responses.

Fat Language: The product is a ticking time-bomb.

Questions: What do you mean? Can you give me an example? Who told you that? What exactly is the problem? How often does it occur? When does it need to be fixed?

Lean Language: The product has several specific obsolescence issues that need to be addressed in the next year, or its functionality will be degraded by ten percent.

14

Aligning Responsibility, Accountability and Authority

This section is confusing, so I have to start with some definitions. The reason it is confusing is that responsibility is sometimes defined as all three of these; people use these terms interchangeably. But for our sake, let's not do that, and we'll define these terms as follows:

Responsibility: The state or fact of having a duty to deal with something.

Accountability: Required or expected to justify actions or decisions.

Authority: The power or right to give orders, make decisions, and enforce obedience.

Think of responsibility, accountability and authority like a three-legged stool. Essentially, you need all three to be successful. Here are a couple of stories of times when a leader did not have all three and what happens. Think about which one was missing.

My friend Sam recently told me about an issue he was having due to experiencing to align responsibility, authority and accountability. As the program manager for a small company, he was responsible for coordinating commitments with customers and then ensuring that the company met its commitments. He was having a hard time getting the software team to investigate an issue that they had previously agreed to do for the customer. They now refused to do it. Sam had to keep making excuses to the customer, who was growing weary, to put it mildly, of all of the delays. So, Sam had trouble executing his job. Then, when things went wrong, he still had the accountability for all of it. Why couldn't he manage this? You can imagine that it did not end well. Which of the three was missing?

Here is another example.

At one organization, I recall a time when we had responsibility for the finances of the organization. We had set up a set of policies and procedures for the group. Everyone agreed to the rules. Yet, at the end of the month, people kept overspending their budgets and apologizing. This went on for months, and it was hindering the long-term objectives of the group. Which of the three was missing?

I had another friend named David who was responsible for an important assignment that was losing money toward the end of the contract. It turned out that he kept getting surprised by cost overruns by a certain department but he was not in charge of that department. He wanted the problem to stop but he felt like he could not control what was happening and felt powerless to change. Which one of the three attributes do you think was missing?

Here is a story about people who focus on their personal careers over the success of the entire company.

In one company, leaders seemed to measure their status by how much Profit and Loss responsibility they had. There was a $4 Billion person, a $1 Billion person and a $500 Million person. The $500 Million person spent a lot of time finding ways to "reorganize" in order to move some of the money from the $1 Billion and $4 Billion people to his organization, or so it seemed. He would come up with all kinds of reasons why this made sense. Perhaps there was some bonus money tied to these numbers, since everyone fiercely defended their turf. The other people now had reason to mistrust him. It seems to me that all of these people work for the same company, and it should not matter, but they would sub-optimize in this way. Imagine what they could do if they spent their creative energies in directions that actually made a difference!

Should we be hard on them? It certainly seems as if they were *incentivized* to behave this way. That's how the accountability was structured. Should we be surprised that people will work in ways that help them get raises, bonuses and promotions?

When things seem complex, ask simple questions like:
- What problem are we trying to solve? This is a great filter question that I use regularly. It provides clarity and helps people to understand intent.
- What opportunity will this create?
- Is there another way to achieve this result in a simpler way?

It is interesting to hear the answers. It might actually be a great idea, or it might expose a hidden agenda. Break out the poop detector, and set it on that three-legged stool.

CHAPTER 14 – ALIGNING RESPONSIBILITY, ACCOUNTABILITY AND AUTHORITY

So how do leaders deal with situations where they don't have all three legs of the stool? There are no easy answers, but I would start with identifying the problem. Build relationships with the people who have the other pieces of the stool. Perhaps establishing a cross-functional team can help. What about finding ways to share leadership or elevate the problem to someone who can help?

In some cases, the right solution might be to walk away or to escalate the conflict. Great leadership can't solve every problem, and sometimes you must take harsh measures to get something done!

15

Developing Confidence

"Fake it until you make it." – Anonymous

I have not always been proud of my thinking or my inner voice. It is as if there is a battle going on, and I am somehow having to choose my way through the battle, the previous choices affecting me as the war goes on. This is not far from the truth of what is actually happening.

Some people seem to have unlimited confidence but chances are that they are also pretending. Everyone has confidence issues from at one point or another. If they don't, they probably have not taken a risk in a while. There is nothing wrong with being in your comfort zone, but leaders who want to advance and grow need to step out and take calculated risks from time to time. That means that the probability of success is less assured. That's ok though. Remember, you achieved much to get here! Take it a step at a time.

The funny thing is that the more you worry about developing confidence the harder it seems to be.

The self-doubter in me would say, who would want to listen to me? Who would want to read my book? Why bother to write it? But that's just a lie -- negative self-talk or self-deception. If I'm in this funk, I am not seeing the world for what it is. I am seeing the world as *I am*. Do you see the difference?

Employers are looking for confident employees, not someone who needs hand-holding. Lack of confidence shines through in interviews, job performance and even in social settings. There are emotional triggers that go with it. Men and women are looking for confident mates. If you lack confidence, you will get passed over. Remember, there will always be someone better looking, smarter and funnier. Just be the best person you can be. That is enough about which to be confident.

Hang around with people who build up your confidence. My parents are good about that. I talk to them often. They remind me of the accomplishments about which I have forgotten. I am not talking about people who are sucking up and stroking your ego. I am talking about authentic people who care about you. Where do you find these people?

Some people have trouble making friends. They are socially awkward, and people don't like to hang around with them. Perhaps they talk about themselves too much. They don't know why they don't have more close friends. Many people are interested but also want a balanced friendship. They want to talk about more than the one person. Other people are more willing to lend an ear, although those people are harder to find. Learning to build friendships by being a good listener and a giver builds confidence.

Here is Aunt Sue's advice about making friends: Be kind. Be nice. Be yourself. Don't pretend to be someone else. People will like you for who you are, or they won't. If they don't, move on. Life's too short to worry about pleasing everybody.

One way to build your confidence is to invest in others and build up their confidence. You are doing something to help someone else. Set an example for others. You never know who is watching you.

It's as if not worrying about your confidence at all is the right way to go. Let it go, and make a difference in the world.

In fact, you've already made a difference. You have impacted people in ways that they may never be able to describe, appreciate or acknowledge. Take confidence in that.

This is not a self-help book. This is a leadership book, and leadership is all about serving others.

16

Moral Courage

"Bad news does not get better with age." — *Not sure who said it first, but lots of leaders have repeated it.*

This might just be one of my favorite chapters in the book because I see so many opportunities for leaders to stand above the rest by sticking to their values, taking decisive action and asking honest questions.

I read an article about a woman in the finance industry who never quite understood the value in the Mortgage-Backed Securities and the Collateralized Debt Obligations (MBS's and CDOs) that were a large part of what brought down the economy in 2007-2008. This was her area of responsibility, and she would not invest in something that she did not fully understand. The other banks were making billions off of these things, and her bank was sitting on the sidelines. I'm sure there was pressure for her to get going. She was probably ridiculed. She received average reviews for years and probably had a lot of self-doubt during that time. But she stuck to it. Her boss supported her. Of course, we know the rest of the story. Many of those other banks were wildly exposed to huge losses, and some of them collapsed. Her bank was just fine, and she became employee of the year. But it took a few years to recognize her.

You won't always get rewarded immediately for your efforts. Some people never see the results. But press on and do the right thing! That's moral courage.

Just because you might be the new guy doesn't mean that you should be afraid to speak up when you are concerned about issues. I had one quality manager tell me of a time that he stopped a billion dollar space program, which was already behind schedule, because he saw systemic issues that needed to be addressed. It was not popular. It was a big deal to stop the program. I am sure that his career flashed before his eyes. Fortunately, they got to work and corrected the issues, putting the program on a better path. Imagine what would have happened if he had not spoken up! Doing the right thing can be tough and lonely.

There are several books and movies I enjoy where you can watch a leader struggle through a tough time standing up for what they believe to be correct. Michael Lewis movies seem to do this, such as "Moneyball" and "The Big Short." I have enjoyed them both and watch them often when I need a shot of moral courage.

Be brave. There were times early in my career where I would have been much better off bringing up important topics instead of letting issues drag on.

Challenges usually don't just solve themselves. I remember one time when we had a seriously bad micromanagement problem when I was in the military. The leader, who was not formally trained in intelligence, would second guess every assessment that the watch floor made. Morale was suffering too, because people felt like their opinions didn't matter. Since morale was low, they sent me in to be the leader's "assistant." It did not take me long to diagnose the problem, since everyone freely told me what was the problem. The question for me was, how do I confront this in a way that doesn't ruin my career? They wanted me to tell the senior officer what the person was doing wrong.

As we had the discussion, I felt my career flash before my eyes as I talked about the serious micromanagement problem. Trust the team. They are college-educated intelligence professionals that get paid good money to assess what's going on. They've been doing this for a long time. I am forever grateful that the officer took the advice well and did not hold it against me. While it seems like a small thing, these little victories will give you confidence for the big ones.

In the end, it was the right thing to do. I was not helping the officer by ignoring the problem or being soft. No one will develop as a leader if he/she does not know that he/she has a problem.

I remember the first time I had to give someone a 60-day lay-off notice. I was dreading it. The person was a good worker and volunteered for just about everything to help make the organization a better place. I must have rehearsed the conversation one hundred times. The employee cried – I did not expect that. I left and felt depressed the rest of the week.

You know what? A couple of years later, she THANKED me! She told me it was the best thing that ever happened to her. You see, the notice motivated her to look for another job, and she found one quickly where she could be successful and enjoyed more than the job she had. In fact, she was quickly promoted. I was blown away by her kind words about a situation we both had thought was so bad.

Sometimes, you have to take the long view of the hard conversations. I find that a lot of leaders are wimps when it comes to hard conversations. Leading is not about being nice all of the time. It is about results in a way that grows people.

Sometimes, there is a great deal of fear in the organization. Many people are afraid to speak up. I got a note recently from a friend who gave me a "badge of courage" for asking the "elephant in the room" question. You know, it's the question on everyone's mind, but it might be seen as career limiting to bring it up. You have to pick your battles and decide for yourself. For me, it was pretty easy to ask because of the way my parents raised me.

One senior VP and mentor told me one time to "forget about the 'chain of command' at the company. Think of the company as one layer deep. You can go talk to anyone. Don't be afraid." I can honestly say that his advice has served me well. In the military, "jumping the chain" can get you in trouble. So this advice may vary depending on where you are working. But I have found that the "chain" often needs to be broken, and the senior leaders need honesty and truth from anywhere in the organization. Going back to a previous chapter, "chain of command" is a poor metaphor. No matter what, do your best to keep people informed. If you decide to go over someone's head, have the courtesy to let them know.

17

Delegating to Others

"If you are working like you used to work, you are doing it wrong."– Marlene Thompkins

When I first became a leader, I took over a team of which I used to be a member. That meant that I knew how to do almost every job on the team. That really helped me in some ways. When other leaders came to me to ask questions, I knew all of the answers. I could step in when someone was sick. I could easily teach people how to do their jobs.

I also had a problem. I was trying to DO their jobs as well as my own. When a hard problem came, I kept it for myself and took care of it. The customer was very happy. But I was not growing the team's skills. I was not asking them to stretch. <u>I was taking responsibility away from them.</u>

After a while, they stopped working as hard. Since I was doing their job, there was less to do! But not for me – I was working twice as hard and enjoying it. I was also wondering why my team was not working as hard as I was. *It turned out that I was creating the environment about which I was complaining.*

One of the best things that happened in my career was when I was asked to move away from that job and lead a multi-disciplined project where I did not have a lot of background. I was forced to delegate and trust. I leveraged the skills that I had, but I could not learn fast enough to do the work of the entire team. I had to realize that my leadership role was not to do all of the work. I had to learn to delegate tasks to the team.

This is a classic leadership development phase. As you transition from follower to leader, there is a natural tendency to work "in your comfort zone." It may even be from one leadership role to another. As you switch jobs, it is naturally uncomfortable that it is new and that you are still learning. Who likes to feel uncomfortable?

I had one boss tell me that, "If you are working like you used to work, you are doing it wrong." I understood what she meant. The new job requires new ways of doing things, new strategies, and a new work rhythm.

Sometimes, you have to get past the idea that the other person will not do the job as fast or as well as you could. That may be true. Pick a task that does not have a tight deadline so that you can develop the person and still get a great product out of the door.

How do you learn to delegate? Practice. Practice. Practice. There's probably some catchy formula, but let's keep it simple.
1. Assign work with an agreed upon completion date. If it is a complex assignment, also agree upon interim milestones. Make it their responsibility to report back to you the progress.
2. Ensure that the person understands the expectations.
3. Check in along the way to see if there are any roadblocks, or if the person needs any help. Do not do the work for them.
4. Review the work at the agreed-upon time.

On the aircraft carrier, the commanding officer had a delegation chart, specifying who was authorized to do what on his behalf. That made a lot of sense. The previous commanding officer wanted <u>everything</u> to go through him, and he tended to get into the details deeply. That worked for him, but the other officers groused about it. The officers got most of the hard stuff done when the commanding officer went on vacation, when he was forced to delegate. It was a mad dash to get work done before he returned!

I used to hear the phrase: You can delegate responsibility, but you can't delegate accountability. What that means is that you can delegate the work, but you are still accountable for the results (as is the delegate). That's true – sort of. One of my goals is to push responsibility and accountability very low in the organization. I remember this paraphrased quote:

"It is extremely important to move responsibility very low in the organization. Your job is not to be working on a project where you can't sleep at night. Your goal isn't to have it so that your project leads can't sleep at night. Your goal is so that nobody sleeps at night. And when nobody sleeps at night, you have pushed responsibility to the proper level." -- Chris Peters

I want everyone to sleep, but I get his message – <u>I want my teammates to have ownership and passion in the quality of work that they do.</u> It is not just a job; it is a great result for a customer in a way that helps others' succeed.

112

18

Be Consistent

"Whether you think you can or think you can't, either way you are right."– Henry Ford

Many people like to have a little structure around their day. At work, sometimes we call it having an operating rhythm or a battle rhythm. Consistency is developing discipline and habits. This helps to ensure that you create time to take care of all of the items for which you and the team are responsible. Here is a sample of something I might set up around my house (we call it a battle rhythm or an operating rhythm):

Daily:
    Affirm the children.
    Eat healthy.
    Exercise.
    Clean pool strainers

Weekly:
    Pay bills.
    Clean pool filters.
    Add chemicals to pool.
    Long bike ride.
    Call parents.

Monthly:
    Clean out car.
    Review budget and finances.

Quarterly:
    Change oil in car.

Annually:
    Develop new resolutions. (Jan)

Set budget. (Jan)
Open the pool. (May)
Service Air Conditioner. (May)
Close the pool. (Oct)

I can tell you that I don't like the structure sometimes, so having something that works for your personality is helpful. Don't be a slave to the structure, and don't ignore important things either. Chores don't do themselves, and procrastination is not your friend.

Consistency requires that you measure your effectiveness, not only what you are doing. Let's say I write a weekly report for my customer. I spend a lot of time on it, but the customer rarely reads it. I think I'm doing a great job, and the customer could care less. If I don't measure effectiveness from others' points of view, I may not be as others' focused as I think I am.

The most important reason to measure things is to reduce uncertainty. Don't measure things just because they can be measured. If there is an easier way to determine something, do that instead. Oftentimes, I see organizations measure the wrong things. They measure what they can, like the number of people who have completed some task, instead of the number of people who learned something new by doing the task, which seems more important to measure.

Leadership excellence in an organization requires that most leaders are heading in the same direction – consistency. If there are two standards, it will confuse people. An example of this <u>not</u> happening occurred one time when a particular employee violated the guidelines on charging with the company credit card. There were very clear disciplinary policies for what to do -- terminate the employee. Well, the manager spent a silver bullet because he really liked the person, who did a good job. The manager spoke and got concurrence with the employee that this needs to NEVER happen again.

After a while, the employee went on travel again, and the same violation occurred. At this point, the manager is past the point of third chances and strongly recommends termination. After a short deliberation, the people operations team, contrary to company policy, recommends a reduced sentence, saying that "some credit card abuse is expected." In response, the management team is confused and proceeds to ask how much credit card abuse is to be expected so that they could inform the rest of the team!

What can you do to improve your level of consistency in the way you lead?

19

Develop Practical Processes

Early in my career, I did not appreciate all of the bureaucracy around the processes and procedures. They seemed like a gigantic book of regulations that kept us from going fast and making decisions. So I often ignored them and did what I thought was right. Most of the time, I did the right thing, but it got me in trouble once in a while. Some of those processes are there to protect the organization from liability or risk. I was inadvertently adding risk that the organization did not want. In fact, they would rather that I *slowed down* and minimized the risk.

So love them or hate them, processes and policies are here to stay. As a leader, you need to embrace them, enforce them, improve them, and remove them.

In order for teams to succeed in a complex environment working together, people often need processes, policies, and instructions. This is a way to communicate how things need to get done. Part of your leadership development will be to read, write, review and approve these processes for your teams. In order to do this, you will need to work with your team to figure out what details need to be written down. Often, I find that this step is overlooked in the face of higher priorities. You also want to avoid situations where only one person on the team can accomplish something. That's why I like the idea of working in teams.

You have to be very careful about how to set up policies and procedures. Do you go for a "one size fits all" approach, or do you allow teams to customize? Both options have pros and cons. Too much process, especially "one size fits all," will burden you with a large bureaucratic mechanism that needs to be sustained.

In one organization, there was a set of robust common processes that were designed for very high quality levels and large programs. I found that the small program I supported would be unaffordable if we tried to comply with all of it. The customer did not need all of the processes. They did not perceive value in it. The product I had to deliver did not have to be perfect – it just had to work about 99% of the time. Sometimes, getting the last 1% is not worth the expense.

Sometimes, we fall into a trap where we decree, in one way or another, that the process is gospel. It must be followed to the letter with no questions asked! While this may be necessary in some critical areas where law or safety is on the line, in other places, it just doesn't make sense. Listen to your teams when they tell you that the process is broken. Also, you don't want people to stop thinking for themselves by relying on the "process."

So the rational leader would try to tailor the process to fit the needs of the team, and, in some cases, it might be easier to land a person on the moon than to get it changed. Sometimes, we seem to convince ourselves into thinking that this policy is gospel and provides the best value for the customer -- until we no longer have a customer. **The bottom line is that you have to drive the process. You cannot let the process drive you.**

If policies are written that incentivize selfish behavior, then it is likely that people will respond that way. For example, some organizations ask managers to collaborate but then measure them by their individual performance. **If the policies invite behaviors that you don't want, then they need to be changed.**

Time Management: There are 4 quadrants of the Eisenhower's Urgent/Important Principle (Covey also has a similar version) in terms of your priorities in general:

Quadrant   Example
1. Urgent and Important – Work that is due in an hour
2. Not Urgent and Important – Documenting the process
3. Urgent and Not Important – Telephone interruptions
4. Not Urgent and Not Important – Responding to Routine e-mails

I find that it is a great goal to ensure that the quadrant 2 work gets done before the quadrant 3 and 4 stuff. **Process improvement work generally falls into the quadrant 2 category. It is often time-consuming, boring and difficult to obtain consensus.** Nevertheless, being a leader sometimes means doing things that you don't enjoy for the betterment of the team and the organization. Do your best to put your passion into it anyway. Remember who you are serving. Try to be helpful and make constructive suggestions to the process owners.

20

Performance Management

"It is important to learn how to have critical conversations."

Performance Management is an important skill to develop as a leader. I have yet to find a perfect system that fairly and consistently evaluates employees. These scores are used to evaluate performance, potential and values. Then the scores often get reused for other purposes, such as salary adjustments, development opportunities, promotions and reductions. This may or may not be a good thing.

One particular skill that is needed and not always promoted by organizations is self-evaluation. What have you done well? What have you not done well? Why? What steps are you taking to improve? **The truth is that no one will hold you more accountable than you can hold yourself.** If you hold yourself to the highest standards, then you are doing great.

I remember the first time I filled out a self-accountability form. It was difficult because I was resisting the idea that I had to expose my flaws for fear that the boss or the organization would hold it against me. This can be a legitimate concern. The workplace has to be a safe environment to be honest, or else people will mostly share the good things and wait to see if anyone finds out about the other things.

I am not a fan of quotas, forced distributions, forced averages, or guidance (which is quotas with a softer name), where we say that we have to have at least 10% or 20% of the people getting the lowest scores. Also, only 10-20% can get the highest scores. Think about the impact to the organization and what this means (refer to the Systems

Thinking chapter). It means that I hired 10-20% of the people really well and 10-20% were poor choices. It means that there will be winners and losers. It means that people will be fighting for the top spots on a team which I need to collaborate and work together. We are actually inviting competition when we should be rewarding collaboration. They might withhold information in order to look better than the other. That seems counter-productive, doesn't it?

My math friends tell me that they ran the classic forced distribution model through a Monte Carlo simulation, and it clearly failed. It did not eliminate the poor performers and also failed to retain the high performers. People learn to "game" the system.

Here's how one scenario works. Once the managers do initial scoring, they get together for a review and start comparing people. It's a tough meeting with everyone fighting for their people and looking for allies. If a manager has only one or two people in the category, he or she has to fight extra hard to get one of the coveted "top performer" spots for deserving people. Others who have more people have already taken the spots. The manager with only one or two reports could be the lone advocate for that person if the person is not well known. Thus the <u>person's scores rest on how well the manager articulates the value the person brought</u> vs. another person (that he probably doesn't even know) in order to convince the other managers to lower the scores on their great people, which they don't want to do.

Someone in the room might declare, somewhat arbitrarily, that a particular skill is more valued than another this year. If this idea is accepted by most, it puts some people at an unfair advantage. It becomes more about how well known a person is, how they perform a certain skill or how much they are respected than it is about overall performance. So that creates a group of people who do their best in future years to become better known rather than to do their best. This also seems counter-productive to me.

I understand what the leaders are trying to do, which is to create differentiation in the work force. They want to know who the stars are and who is struggling. The system is just broken. There has to be a better way that aligns an organization's values, and I think there is. I'm still experimenting with it.

If you learn to apply performance management correctly, then there should be **no surprises** at the end of the year. Everyone will agree upon the score. That is my goal – no surprises. If I set up the goals correctly and put the right self-accountability environment in place where we talk regularly about performance, then the person will be able to self-report how they are doing. They will be the ones reporting against the standard. We will be able to adjust throughout the year. All of this takes time to set up, but I would say that it is well worth the investment to go slow early to avoid problems later.

There are many books about how to have critical conversations. It is an important skill to learn, and I find that many leaders struggle with it. It is something that must be practiced. Rather than spending a short amount of time talking about it here, I would rather point you to other experts that will help you develop this skill, such as the "Crucial Conversations" series.

I find that many leaders do not like to have hard conversations. They can be messy. They take more time and are emotionally draining. There needs to be more evidence. It would be easier to give the person a score that they will accept and move on. To me, the person who takes the easy way out is a leader who is not doing his or her job. Leadership is not for wimps.

Is there a critical conversation that you have been avoiding? Why? What are you afraid of? If you really cared about the person, wouldn't you want to tell them what they need to know in order to improve? Do you ask your leader for feedback?

Part III
Advanced
Leadership Topics

FRANTIC LEADERSHIP

21

Changing Culture

"The pain of doing nothing is worse than the pain of doing something wrong." – Anonymous coworker

One of the questions people often ask me is: How do you change the culture of an organization? This is an important question, and we should break it down a little.

First, there is an implied need that something in the organization needs to be fixed. But what? We don't know what, so we invented a word called "culture." We use it liberally. When I used to talk to leaders about fixing the culture, they would laugh me out of the room. It is too nebulous to fix the culture, they would tell me. It's like trying to cure world hunger. In other example, someone said, "Culture is organic; it will fix itself." Problems, if left unchecked, generally don't fix themselves.

This need may or may not be acknowledged by the leadership. Sometimes leaders think they have tried everything and are just convinced that it cannot be fixed, at least not by them.

In organizations that are very political (where people seem to be jockeying for position, for example), sometimes people force out the leaders who most exemplify the values that the organization claims are most important. It is very demoralizing for the workers to see that the leaders who speak their mind or challenge the status quo are summarily told to walk the line, and keep quiet or else. It makes it clear that the organization actually values something else more.

Chapter 21 CHANGING CULTURE

Here is an example of a time when I misread the environment. I first joined a particular company in a period of transition. They had recently merged with another company, and cash was very tight. My first impressions of the company culture was, "we have no overhead money. Don't bother to ask." So if I needed anything at work, I usually found a way to buy it myself. I learned to work ultra-lean, never asking for anything for years, as it left an indelible impression on me. Don't bother to ask. When I became the manager a few years later, I told my boss about some of the challenges on the team, and he suggested that we spend some overhead to solve it. I said, surprised, "We have some of that?" He just laughed at me -- of course we do. You mean to tell me that we could have solved this problem six months ago? Yes. I felt kind of foolish at the time, but I learned something that I hope you will take with you. Be careful what you say and how you say it, as it leaves imprints on the hearts and minds of others. If I had only heard, "don't bother to ask until the next fiscal year" then I would have better understood his message. Instead, I labeled him as "Mr. No." I had conditioned myself not to approach him on that subject.

When you are a leader on a new team, you have to accept the mistakes of the past. Although I was new, the team was not! They had plenty of "culture" that they were carrying around. In one job, I seemed to be responsible for not only my actions but also for the all of the bad decisions managers have made in the past! One employee told me that he liked to make fun of management because they made it so easy to do so. In a weird way, employees were happy that the team failed because it justified that their complaints had merit. (Think about that for a second. If I am happy when the company who pays my salary is failing, then something is twisted!) Managers can be easy targets. Sometimes we don't listen and find creative ways to fail to accept responsibility in the name of responsibility. It is incredible how the human mind can twist the truth to be justified.

I had one colleague who invented a very robust computer system fifteen years ago. Five years later, the management outsourced the work to a subsidiary company. The inventer was very upset and claimed that he was concerned that the subsidiary company would not have the skills. But the truth came out years later. He was most upset that the management "took away his baby." As I would approach him for advice on how to improve the tool, he would not help me or put his full energy into it, and I never understood why until he explained it that way. Imagine how you would feel if someone ripped your life's passion away from you! I get it. He was hurting. How do you think he would have described the culture?

We can do all sorts of irresponsible things in the name of responsibility. It may have been the right business decision at the time. In hindsight, I would say no, but it is unfair to play armchair quarterback.

The competitors are coming. The challenges are coming. It is a matter of time. I saw an article describing a group of employees as "The Frozen Middle," suggesting that the executives were good. The new people were fine. It's that stubborn group in the middle that won't change! Do you think this is the whole truth? Think about what we have learned. First, note the "Red Flag" of labelling them "The Frozen Middle." It is a blame, which suggests inward mindset. You can't fix culture from an inward mindset, because you will invite more inward mindset from the very people you are trying to change.

There was this one place I worked where "Red is Dead," meaning that the person who put a red stoplight on the chart was going to get it, was the norm. This particular leader would measure <u>in great detail deep in the organization</u> and want to ensure that nothing was "Red" on the stoplight charts across his whole organization. People were afraid of him. It was a "get it done at all costs" mentality, even if it was wrong; so long as we don't have to put Red on the chart! People would hide the truth and then hide behind the poor guy who was being honest and taking the "beatings." The "beatings" meant more meetings, more charts, more status reporting, and more recovery plans. People should be asking for help, but if the "help" came in the form of more work that was not helpful, no thank you. It was abusive.

At another place, people would yell during meetings and think in terms of their own problems. He who had the money to help did not see the need to fund those who did not unless it was to the letter of the law. It was very selfish thinking. The other guy without the money ended up spending much of his time justifying his existence and resenting the people with the money. In the meantime, nobody was paying as much attention to the right results or the customer. There was much fear in the organization. People worried about how they were seen by others, (e.g., if the employee survey scores aren't high enough, or if there are negative comments in the survey). When you step back, you knew something had to change, but what?

When something bad happens, some organizations have a tendency to overreact and fall off the horse in the other direction. For example, if one person abuses the company credit card policy, then all spending is revoked for everyone, creating all kinds of unnecessary bureaucracy and wasted time. If one person does something wrong in travel, now travel has to be approved by the vice president. You get the idea. Eventually, we hope that level heads will prevail.

Culture does not exist. One day I was complaining about the "culture" during a class about conflict transformation given by Chad Ford. It was an amazing class. Anyway, Chad called me out by saying to me something I had never considered. **"There is no such thing as culture, Christian."** Huh??? Do you mean to tell me that everyone is wrong???

He explained that *"culture" is whatever I need it to be when I need to be justified for all of the wrongs around me.* It is constantly shifting. If it is constantly changing. **If it is constantly changing, even in my own head, then there really is no such thing.** "Culture" is great justification.

That knocked me off balance, so I started an opinion poll. I asked a large group of people what the culture was like in the organization. I asked thirty people and got thirty different answers. There were some prevailing themes. The crux of it was that if the person questioned had an inward mindset toward the organization, the answer was generally a blaming adjective, like bureaucratic, uncaring or toxic. If the person had an outward mindset, the answer to the culture question was about possibilities or values, such as innovative or exciting. Even more interesting, when I had an inward mindset when asking these questions, I was actually irritated when others did not agree with me!

So I am no longer on a quest to change "culture." Instead, I am on a quest to change mindset, which drives everything else.

So here are the 3 steps to improving large organizations (based on the work by the Arbinger Institute and discussed in the book "The Outward Mindset"):

1. Shift mindsets outward. (Most organizations are not aware of this step and thus skip it.)

   Some experts think that there are alternatives to Mindset change, such as "Emotional Intelligence," "Five Dysfunctions of a Team," "7 Habits," and many other hot leadership programs. I have found that they fall short. They might give the organization a short boost, but we are interested in LASTING change. I think of analogy: "If you give a man a fish, he eats for a day. If you teach a man to fish, he eats for a lifetime." **I am talking about a permanent Mindset shift across contiguous work teams.**

2. Turn objectives and behaviors outward.

   Once Mindsets are shifted outward, all sorts of objectives and behaviors become possible for others. People are more creative.

3. Turn systems and processes that support these people outward. (Otherwise it will undermine the work you did in steps 1 and 2.)

Companies and organizations who have followed this model have outperformed their peers. I would contend that Mindset is an excellent predictor of success, certainly much better than "culture."

This is not trivial nor easy to do – so I would recommend getting advice from experts at Arbinger, instead of trying to invent this in your organization.

Is there space to improve "successful" organizations? If it's not broken, why fix it? I hear that a lot. In the global economy, he who is not improving is falling behind. It is no different personally than it is organizationally. Eventually, someone will come along who is faster, leaner, and smarter. Why allow your organization to stagnate?

22

Communication

"e-mail does not equal communication." —Marlene Thompkins

An astute reader might wonder if this is really an *advanced* leadership topic. I think so because many leaders either neglect this important skill or fail to incorporate enough communication into his/her operating rhythm.

Communicating is about connecting with people, not just about sending a message. This is a little bit complex. There is a sender, the sender's state of mind, a transmission medium, a receiver, and the receiver's state of mind, or mindset. An effective communicator will also invite a mindset change.

State of mind is very important, both yours and theirs. Ask a progressive liberal to read George W. Bush's memoir. Ask a Libertarian to watch MSNBC. No matter what good information might be there, it was a bad from the start because the receiver was not open to the message.

What's worse is that the news channels are incredibly biased. If you listen to what they choose to cover, it is obvious that they are trying to shape your thinking (often in an inward way that generates ratings) instead of presenting facts in an unbiased way.

Chapter 22 COMMUNICATION

I used to watch a show on Fox News called Hannity and Colmes (featuring Sean Hannity and Alan Colmes.) The news network, notoriously biased toward conservative causes, liked to position themselves as offering alternative viewpoints from the equally notoriously liberally-biased media. So in a sense, Alan Colmes was the "token liberal" on the network. (He would get verbally hammered a lot, and he took it well.)

Here's the problem -- two extremists talking about an issue is far from "fair and balanced." They might ask a question like, "Don't you agree that so-and-so is a hater?" Remember what I said about labels. Therefore, I don't much care for the news anymore.

Any "fair and balanced" TV show, meeting, or discussion would be one about curiosity, about being open to win-win scenarios, about learning why people are passionate, about how I might be wrong, and about how each side has some merit at times. Great leadership is about bringing people together, not tearing them apart. I am personally disgusted by the rancor and tactics of the political system in the United States. If I were President, I would focus on the results that the country needs instead of trying to meet a political agenda of one party or another. As a nation, that's what we would talk about. We'd bring in experts to help us solve problems, and solicit suggestions from the public. We have an urgent set of needs upon which to focus. Our focus would largely remain on the "Top 20" instead of following the news cycles. We, as a nation or community, should be driving the media, not the other way around! In other words, we should be acting, not reacting.

If someone prepares you ahead of time to "listen for the flaw in the statement," then that is what you will find. Conversely, if someone says, "listen for the opportunity in this statement," then that is what you will find. The leadership must be considerate of this in any communication plan. If you do not care about the people receiving the message, then it is very possible that they not only will not get your message but also will not even care about you or your message! In fact, they will look for all sorts of things that are wrong with your message. Their starting point will be to find out what is wrong with you, and you have to overcome that.

Communication media can come in many varieties. The important thing to keep in mind is to select the right medium for the message. For example, I try never to communicate bad news via e-mail. Bad news is usually complex and requires more interactive forms of communication. Remember that with any communication media, there is an inherent medium error rate. That means that the media method is not 100% effective in communication. In fact, e-mail and texting are media that have the highest medium error, yet we seem to use them most because they is convenient.

Here are some general guidelines that, if we followed them, I think we would be better off. Look for the latest technologies to help you better communicate. Things like webcasts, FaceTime, Skype for Business, Blogs, Wikis, and much, much more all have their place. Don't be afraid to try something new. Web cameras are handy and helpful at times. Think about how they can accelerate communication or collaboration. Imagine what could happen if you could get the team onboard 20% faster or if you could incentivize the right behaviors faster.

Different generations like to communicate in different ways. Be sensitive to that. Texting and Instant Messaging have taken on a life of their own. Some people love it, and others prefer more personal touches.

E-mail is probably most popular today, but it's also one of the most inefficient methods to communicate effectively. There are ways to do e-mail better though.

- Don't send a long e-mail with a complicated message unless it is absolutely necessary.
- Keep the emotion out of your e-mails. Focus on facts and data. Use this rule of thumb: Do you want this e-mail to be discoverable in the future for the world to see?
- In order to avoid clutter and help my readers know which e-mails are important, I use the Navy messaging system of importance (Flash, Priority, Routine) and direction (Action or Information). I also color code my e-mails using Outlook to know which are for me (red), which are to me and others (blue), and which are "cc" only (green). That helps me prioritize and respond to them.
- If someone sends you an emotionally charged e-mail or text, you are not obligated to respond in the same way. First, try not to be so hard on them. Some people are passionate and wear their hearts on their

sleeves. They have not learned this etiquette. Sometimes a phone call or an in-person visit is a better way to respond. Some people react by responding to a nasty e-mail the same way. While it might make you feel better, it often does not help and reflects poorly upon you.

- Good news can be shared in public. Bad news is delivered in person and in private. Don't gossip about it. Have discretion.
- Don't over distribute information. The "reply to all" should be used sparingly, not automatically.

Another truism I learned along the way is that e-mail does not equal communication. Some people think that communication occurred just because they hit the send button. E-mails can be filtered, lost, buried, misunderstood or never read. If it is really important, follow it up with a phone call. Be deliberate about your communication. Have a plan. Use many media methods, including social media. Don't be afraid to try something new.

Every place I have ever worked has had, for the most part, great leadership at the top. I enjoy listening to the passion, vision and experience of these people. Sometimes that passion did not translate down to the middle management or the workers. It would be easy to watch this great initiative get sandblasted by busy middle managers who had to implement this program on their teams. Without understanding the "why," they would not be as enthusiastic about it. By the time it reached the workers, it seemed like yet another lame-brained idea. This is why some leaders have to do their own public relations campaign in order to get their message to the workers.

There are a few leaders that I have really admired over the years because they were such great communicators. While everyone has strengths and weaknesses, I can tell you this – great leaders must also be great communicators. One particular leader seemed to have a jet pack on his career. Besides a ridiculous amount of energy, passion and discipline, he also had a great communication plan. A communication plan is a great way to be proactive about the way you plan to deliver your message. He segmented his receivers and targeted different groups with different messages. He practiced his communicating until he was comfortable in front of large audiences, news media, corporate investors and the Board of Directors. He knew that he had to keep his messages clear and concise, and he knew his stuff. If someone asked him a question, he had an answer most of the time. He was also smart enough to realize two things. One was that other people might know more than him, so he involved his team to answer some of the detailed questions. Second, his getting them involved was part of his development plan for them. He was supporting them so that they would feel comfortable when it was their turn to lead one of these sessions.

This leader was very consistent as well. He made communication a high priority and believed the more the team knew what was happening, the better. He was not afraid to try new technologies, including social media techniques. He had a weekly blog on which teammates could express their opinions. He read them himself and often responded. He had quarterly interactive webcasts and presentations. He shared his personal accountability scorecard, including the topics where he needed help. He also sent personal e-mails on a regular basis and spent significant time to visit customers and teammates. He did his best to live the values that he believed and enjoyed finding others to showcase as examples of these values. The best part about his communication was that he was accessible to the masses. It was not just a one-way communication.

It amazed me when a large group of people said in the annual survey that they did not know where the organization was going. It was not because the leader did not try to connect with them. I can't think of what more he could have done (within reason). I would suggest that their response was probably more because the receivers were not really listening or were listening with the wrong mindset.

That is a big part of the leadership challenge – **to connect positively with people who have issues.** We all have issues. We've all been misunderstood, mistreated, and wronged in our one way or another. If we bring this with us when trying to listen to someone, we just might miss the message.

When I think about developing a proactive communication plan, I quickly realize that it is not enough to communicate well. I have to develop a proactive caring plan; then, communication planning is a sub-element of the caring plan. In other words, a good communication plan with a poor implementation plan will only serve to discredit.

Chapter 22 COMMUNICATION

Sometimes, we get the communication correct, but the message is not believed. There are many politicians that are putting out great communication but do not garner additional votes simply because people do not have trust that the communication is truth, or people get the impression that the politician does not care about them. Many people mistakenly think that the solution to these problems is more communication. Unfortunately, the problem is deeper, at the mindset level; therefore, the solution must also be deeper. Any other solution, besides communication, at the behavioral level will fail for the same reasons.

Communication is such an important topic that people write entire books about it, and many companies have full-time professionals managing the brand and the communications. I like to think that I am a good communicator, but a recent experience taught me that I have more work to do. I was presenting to a director in my company, and I could tell that I was just not connecting with him. He was constantly interrupting me out of frustration, and I was speaking over his head on technical matters. I was not effectively answering his questions. He is a pretty smart guy, and we have a good relationship. I was surprised when I was having trouble. He does not have the same degree as mine, and I was doing my best to take the jargon out and keep it simple, and I was still failing. I appreciated a peer telling me that it is my responsibility to fix this. I wanted the other person to change – to get what I was saying, but that really wasn't fair nor was it the reality.

If I am having trouble communicating, then it is my problem to resolve.

23

Applying Technology to Leadership Challenges

Any time that an author writes about new technology, you can be assured that it will be obsolete in about three years and maybe sooner. So I will try to hit some high points about some common guidelines I use regarding technology and how to use it to make us more efficient. This is far from an exhaustive list.

If I spend all day in front the computer screen looking at e-mail, then I am probably not doing something else that is more important. It is easy to get sucked in by the technology. Remember the Eisenhower "Urgent/Important diagram" in chapter 19.

Keep it simple. People often try to build something more complex than it needs to be in order to impress other people. I recommend keeping it simple. Add no more complexity than necessary. It will be easier to maintain most of the time.

Productivity. I like to create one-page quick link pages for the things I have to find regularly on the intranet. If you add up how much time is saved one minute at a time not looking up stuff, it adds up to close to a day more efficient by the end of the year. If you can multiply this for your entire team, the savings multiply too.

Innovation. There have been several advances in technology lately that really are game changers. One is the widespread availability of cloud computing. Amazon, HP, Evernote, Dropbox, and others have developed all sorts of tools that make starting a company much easier by essentially leasing space from their infrastructure instead of buying your own. You have to work through the security issues, but that will get better. This is a game changer because it is a disruptive technology, like the cell phone was to the landline phone.

Another disruptive technology is data analytics. Much of the actual analytical parts of this have been around for years, although some techniques are relatively new. Thanks to cloud computing and faster computing power, the ability to analyze data quickly is a game changer. Machine learning algorithms and artificial intelligence are here to stay and have the potential to disrupt in a big way. For example, I was looking at Kaggle.com today going through tutorials about trying to predict who would survive the Titanic disaster using Machine Learning algorithms in the R programming language.

Additive manufacturing, or 3-D printing, is really catching on and creating all sorts of opportunities. They are easy enough to build in your own home as a hobbyist. They are even trying to 3-D print human body parts, cars, airplane parts and houses.

General Administrative Tasks. You will need to become familiar with tools such as Microsoft Office, which includes Word, PowerPoint, Excel, Project, Access and more. The more you get familiar with these tools, the more effective and efficient you will be. These general purpose tools can solve a whole host of simple problems.

Collaboration. There are all sorts of ways to share information with teams scattered about that was not available even a few short years ago. Collaborative workspaces are very helpful. Group sharing and crowdsourcing are very popular now.

Tracking Actions. You can keep it simple and use someone like Microsoft Excel or Project to keep track of actions, or build a more elaborate tool yourself. The important thing is to get things done and not to forget about things. I am kind of old fashioned and still use a notebook.

Managing Risks. I have yet to see a good generic risk management tool, but it would not be that hard to adapt using Excel or Access if needed. If you have one that you like, let me know!

If you have technology ideas, let me know at christian@franticleader.com! Send me the leadership challenge and the technology suggestion. We will keep your ideas up to date on our web site!

24

Building Your Team

"Be willing to have contrarians and critics on your team so that you are not drinking your own bath water." – Christian Hasselberg (adapted using the idiomatic phrase)

There is a difference between "holding them accountable" and "creating a culture where accountability thrives." The difference is revolutionary. (Arbinger Institute)

Whenever I took on a new job, I had feelings of excitement that created energy for me. I would get to meet and work with new people, taking on new challenges to fulfill my customers' mission. That's day one. **Remember what this feels like!** You may need to reach back to this feeling when times get tough.

It is very rare that you get to pick your team from scratch. Generally, you inherit the people on your team, and you need them to be successful in order to achieve results and in order for you to succeed.

One of your first orders of business is to meet your people, get to know them and listen to them carefully. Unfortunately, I have found that many leaders skip this step. The people on your team will tell you all kinds of things that you need to know to be successful. Some of them might resent you from the get go, because they might have been passed over for the chair in which you are now sitting or for any number of other reasons. The most professional ones will get past that. Others will struggle for a while.

Ask them and yourself: what are their career goals and aspirations? How can I help them remove barriers and roadblocks? If they could change one thing, what would it be? What suggestions do they have? In order to <u>retain your credibility</u>, you need to follow up on each and every suggestion and idea.

One of the things that you may have to get past is that they may have shared these things with the last five bosses they had as well, and "nothing was ever done about it." That may or may not be true, but it really doesn't matter. You are here now, and you are listening. Sometimes, I've had to apologize to them for the way that they have been treated by OTHER managers. I have been labeled as "one of them." I have found that the cost of a sincere apology is very low. That sincere apology helps provide space for people to forgive and move on with their lives.

When you get the opportunity to bring people on, it is a great opportunity to improve your team! Take that responsibility very seriously. I think a lot of people do not hire well. This is an important skill to have.

First of all, I think that many people frame the job descriptions in a way that is unhelpful. Most jobs talk about what the person has to do and what skills and experiences are required. That seems like a good start. But several things are missing. First, what results does the position need to achieve? Isn't that more important that what the person does? If you tell a person the results, it gives them the space to figure out what they need to do. Second, I find that hiring a person with the right mindset and motivation is far more important than hiring a person with experience and skills. I seem to be in the minority here, but I have found that I can invest in a motivated person and do better than if I hire a person with experience and an inward mindset. Don't get me wrong – you still need experience and wisdom. However, I find that over-emphasis on those skills and experiences can hurt. I want to see potential in prospective hires. How are they going to make the team better? Finally, I think of "fit" on the team, in terms of diversity and inclusion. If a superstar is going to disrupt the whole team, then he or she might still be a bad fit for the team. Find a different place for him or her.

I like to spend time with candidates and be very curious. Ask a lot of questions that brings out the candidate's personality, mindset, motivations, skills, and experience. Ask a lot of open-ended questions.

Don't forget that they also have choices in employment, so you may need to sell your organization to them as well. Why should they want to work for you? What will you do for them that no other leader can provide?

Frantic Sidebar – Top-Heavy vs. Balanced Organizations

I work in a very cyclical industry that hires people based on government budget cycles, which vary considerably based on external factors. This causes the organization to be lop-sided from time to time. Over many years, hard-working people were promoted based on years of service, kind of like a reward for the hard work. Alternatively, some people were promoted for a leadership role but were moved to other jobs over time without ever losing pay or position. So there are times when a team is top-heavy and too expensive. I prefer the way the Navy did it, where they analyzed what was needed (billets) and staffed to that level. Their motto was, "No Billet? No Body!"

Too many managers? Let's say there is a big cross-functional problem among many teams. One idea might be to hire a senior manager to solve the big problem. After all, the problem spans across multiple business units and functions, and everyone else is either too busy or incapable of solving the problem. So the solution to the problem, to hire another manager to fix what the other managers could not, adds to the problem. Over time, there is a plethora of senior managers, and the manager to employee ratio gets too high.

So what's my point? Sometimes, it would be better to create the right accountability with the team that you have than to keep hiring more people. I remember this one time my friend Daren had a small implosion inside his company. Several people quit all at once, and it came out that a certain leader was responsible. All that was left of a team of six was a part-time person. Daren met with the part-time person and developed a plan. After a few weeks, the two of them figured out how to do all of the necessary work with only the one part-time worker! The larger team was creating all sorts of process and bureaucracy that was keeping them employed and, ultimately, perceived to be of little value.

Diversity. Be willing to have contrarians and critics on your team so that you do not have "groupthink." Don't just hire people like you. Hire smarter and different types of people with different backgrounds and experiences that will do the jobs needed with enthusiasm.

Sometimes the hiring processes and policies in place have unintended consequences. In an effort to be more efficient, we asked the hiring managers to put in "minimum qualifications" type questions to help screen applicants. If you answered anything but "yes" to every question, then it was the hiring manager's opinion that you were not qualified for the job. In principle, this makes sense, but in practice something else occurred. Hiring managers often asked the wrong questions. For example, for a job as a supplier manager, the question was, "Do you have experience as a supplier manager?" That eliminates many qualified candidates that have never been a supplier manager before. For example, a finance manager looking for a rotation opportunity would probably be very qualified. They know the deeper, fiduciary questions to ask. In another example, the questions asked whether the person had fifteen years of experience in finance. That type of question regarding quantifiable years of experience lent itself to people who had been in the same discipline for many years as opposed to people who rotated around in their careers. Also, who says a year of experience is equal between two people? If we had a potential candidate with fourteen years of experience, they would be either not be considered or would have to resort to lying in order to be considered, which is never a good idea. This frustrates job seekers who seem to be shut out of opportunities.

I would suggest an alternative. Ask behaviorally based questions, like: "Do you have the capability to…" or "Are you willing to…" Avoid questions like, "Have you ever…" or "Do you have xx years of experience in xxx?" What are you really trying to determine?

Over time, you will develop your ability to read people and develop emotional intelligence. A good friend of mine told me that <u>if you want to know what a person is like, listen to how the person talks about others</u>. This is very good advice, and it challenges me every day to think better, to live better, and to talk better about others. It is a journey.

I have had several instances where another manager asked me to take one of their people. Early in my career, I accepted these people based on the manager's word. No more. Some managers were passing around their "problem employees" instead of acting to correct the issues. Lesson Learned – always perform your due diligence, and insist on getting the information you need to make a good decision. A bad hire can take years to fix.

In conclusion, hiring new people is a bit of a challenge because it is a high stakes decision, and it can really help a team turn a corner to become high performing. Take your time and make the right decision. Be sensitive to the process, and always be in compliance with legal and regulatory guidelines. Within the rules, there is room to ask your questions, and make the best decision.

25

Dealing with Disappointment

"When things go wrong, am I quick to blame others, or do I take responsibility for my role in the problem and invite others to do the same?" – adapted from the Arbinger Institute

"Things are never as bad as they seem and never as good as they seem." -- Jeff Wieringa, Harper Lee, Troy Aikman, and probably others

What do you do when people don't understand or don't buy into what you are trying to do? It can be very frustrating and lonely when you are the only person who can visualize the results for which you are hoping. It can be filled with self-doubt. You can get labeled Chicken Little, the crazy person, or the annoying one. One thing I would recommend is to keep being true to your message, but you might want to consider refining or reframing the message to help people see from where you are coming. Also, don't be afraid to re-evaluate whether you are wrong. It might help. Sometimes, you just have to let events play out, watch the consequences and avoid the urge to say, "I told you so."

One thing I regret is that I over-reacted to being mistreated early in my career. When I was in the Navy, they instituted a ratings quota system, when only so many people could get the highest marks, second highest, and so on. I was newly promoted in the rank of Lieutenant, and review time came. I put my best effort into my job, but I received the lowest ratings of my career. The rationale I heard from the boss was that I was new to the rank and that the other guys needed the higher scores for their careers, which was true. They were good officers too. I liked them. The commander who had to give me the crap news just told me to keep doing what I was doing, and I hadn't done anything wrong. I was upset at the organization for making an imperfect rating and ranking system – very upset. While I was calm on the outside, work in the Navy was never the same for me after feeling betrayed like that. That, along with the decision to cut retirement benefits for my year group, made the decision to leave the service easier for me. At the time, I was the personal briefer for a 3-star general, which was a great, coveted job. When the general found out that I was leaving, he personally asked me to reconsider, which was a nice gesture. Unfortunately, an Army general can't fix the Navy.

I'd like to think that I grew out of this, but I did not upon receiving news of my first demotion. The organization called it something more friendly-sounding, but we all knew what was happening. I struggled with the injustice of it for about a year. I had excellent performance reviews but that did not seem to matter. Setbacks like this can happen to anyone, and when you aspire to leadership excellence, it can certainly shake your self-confidence.

Similar things occur all of the time. In all industries, efforts around diversity, inclusion and breaking "glass ceilings," which somehow get translated into protected class diversity, are gaining momentum. This is meant to offset previous years where those protected classes were not considered for advancement systematically. Either way, it's an unfair system, where we are trying to right the wrongs of the past. People get hurt.

I am strongly in favor of a diverse and inclusive workforce. I have seen many examples where a diverse team beat the pants off of other teams. I may not be a genius by myself, but add just one smart person from a diverse background, and our collective IQ will get us there.

Career setbacks are a part of life, both for you and for your friends. Sometimes, I had to be the person getting the bad news, other times I watched others receive the bad news, and sometimes I had to deliver the bad news. I watched my father get hosed on a few occasions. He then had trouble finding work in his fifties due to age discrimination, and it left scars on my mindset about companies, loyalty and fairness.

What can I say? Life is not fair, but **I am still required and am being paid to do my best.** It would be very easy to use these injustices as an excuse to do less than my best, and I have from time to time. However, the sooner I get past that and press on with my life – the better. I wish I had a secret formula for you to not get angry at injustice, but I don't. But I do know that leaders who whine and complain invite more whining and complaining. Be a good example!

I have a friend named Dave who told me that the organization was trying to get rid of him. He said he went from "content with work" to "job hunting mode" within twenty minutes. He had developed an ability to adjust quickly. I hope we can learn from him. When dealing with disappointment, live your values.

Is there any disappointment of which you have to let go? Frankly, the only person you are hurting by not forgiving and moving on is yourself.

When something goes wrong in the organization, there is a natural tendency to point the finger at the people most responsible. I would question how helpful that really is. All we've done is separate ourselves from them. Keep in mind, if one part of the organization is failing, so am I, as I am a part of the organization. If my employee fails, then so did I as a leader. Here is an alternative thing to do. Ask yourself, how am I responsible for what happened? Was there anything that I did or should have done, no matter how small, that contributed to the situation? Take responsibility for that and go do it. Invite others to do the same thing.

When things go wrong, am I quick to blame others, or do I take responsibility for my role in the problem and invite others to do the same?

When faced with injustice, how can I find ways to stay the course and be true to my values?

26

Systems Thinking - Solving Complex Problems

"Rarely are things as simple as they appear."

What is systems thinking? **Systems thinking is the process of understanding how things which may be regarded as systems influence one another within a complete entity, or larger system.** (Wikipedia) One important discipline that has emerged in importance is systems engineering, which is an interdisciplinary field of engineering that focuses on how to design and manage complex engineering systems over their life cycles. (Wikipedia) Do not let the "engineering" term scare you. It's not that hard to become a better systems thinker. One of the books I recommend, "Thinking in Systems," by Donella Meadows, provides a great overview that should be required reading for everyone. It helps people be more informed and make better decisions.

Disagreements can occur because people do not understand the benefits of systems thinking. There are many examples of this. Let's suppose that I think we should find a way as a nation to provide free college for everyone who achieves some eligibility. That sounds like a great idea and would likely garner support. I certainly do not like the idea of indebting our college students at such a young age, especially our lower paid ones such as teachers, with so much debt that it will take years and years to pay off. These people pursued the dream and now are stuck. Some of them are still living with their parents in order to pay off debt.

Who is to blame? Ultimately, it's the person who chose to assume the debt. That makes them most responsible. The person bought into what some advisor, parent, or conventional thinking recommended. The price of college is rising faster than inflation. This is the way the system works. There is a limited amount of scholarships and financial aid available. In some respects, it is a flawed system.

But is "Who is the blame" the right question? <u>If we focus on blame, then we are not focused on solutions, and this is a complex problem worth consideration.</u>

Is giving away free education the right answer? It seems to work in a few smaller countries. Can it work the in the U.S.? Let's think about it. There is no such thing as a free lunch. The money has to come from somewhere to finance this program. Some people have said things like, "We'll just tax the rich. They aren't paying enough anyway. They have plenty to spare."

That may sound reasonable on the surface, but it also has its consequences. In some respect, we would be directing the wealth transfer between one person and another, theoretically for the common good. Of course, the program will need to be managed, so it will come with overhead costs and bureaucracy. <u>Let's think about the person who would pay for it.</u> That person has fewer resources to start a company, spend money on boats, or contribute to charities. So what, right? So those charities will suffer. The company that could have been the next Apple creating billions in taxes will not get created. The boat and customer home builders will lose their jobs. What about the student that got something for free? <u>Something given is not as valued as something earned.</u>

This is just the second order systems impacts. You then have to think about the impact of those events happening! The unemployed worker has to find a job and collects unemployment. The government has less tax revenue in the future. The charity can no longer provide the level of support to needy people. The entitled student might be very appreciative or might expect the world to give them everything.

Now, this is a fictitious example that you might think is extreme. The bottom line is: <u>you should think about the impacts of things before you develop strong, uneducated opinions.</u> We all do this, so don't be too hard on yourself. We can't know everything, but we think about systems impacts.

Can you think of other ideas to solve this problem? What about asking for more donations? What about more work for school programs? How about addressing the cost of college by disrupting the college model with technology? What about advising more students to pay-as-you-go, or find other ways to pay for college? There are lots of things we can do to help. It is only limited by our mindset and our imagination.

Corruption and fraud are our biggest enemies, not the rich or poor. My friends – warfare is not the answer. We need to be responsible and work together. Suppose a group of fishermen (or fisherwomen) take one more fish from the ocean than their share each day. They justify it – it's just one more fish in the ocean. Surely, it won't matter. But it does. It has to. Eventually, it gets harder and harder to get a quota, and the quotas will get lowered to preserve what is left. Eventually, some people have to stop fishing. This is an example of a shared resource. It is up to each of us to be responsible and ethical to a far higher standard than the law or policy.

What caused the 2008 financial crisis? There have been lots of books and movies that attempt to provide "the reason." You might even buy into a theory. The democrats might blame "Wall Street greed," and the Republicans might blame "government regulation changes." Do you know what I think? They are both right and wrong. It's a complex system. There were many contributing elements. First and foremost, Osama bin Laden attacking our country in 2001 created certain economic conditions that disrupted the system. The economy stopped. Interest rated plummeted to spur investment. That would not have happened if the government leadership had acted more boldly upon the indications, warnings and previous attacks in Saudi Arabia, Kenya and Tanzania years earlier. It did not surprise me one bit that Bin Laden attacked the United States. I saw his organization increase its capabilities over several years but never could have predicted the timing. Why did Bin Laden do what he did? I can go on and on. These are complex systems, and people are part of systems.

We do our best to model systems in different ways. Some people do not have adequate tools to model systems, so they just do their best to understand what the "pundits" say in the media. If you have a grasp on systems thinking, you will be better equipped to think for yourself as a leader.

So what should you take away from this chapter? Rarely are things as simple as they appear. **Systems thinking is extremely important in decision making.**

Systems Thinking and Risk. Our collective ability to identify and measure risk appropriately stinks. At work, we think about risks, issues and opportunities. For our purposes, risks are bad things that might happen. Issues are bad things that have already happened, and opportunities are good things that we'd like to happen. We develop risks using an if/then model, such as, "If the oil rig erupts, then there will be an economic catastrophe." We place a probability of occurrence and consequence of occurrence on each one. Then, based on the perceived levels, we develop plans to avoid, transfer, mitigate or accept the risk. Opportunities and issues are managed similarly.

So that's the system as we understand it today. Here's where I think the system breaks down. We treat each risk as if it is independent, but it is not. People interact with systems and processes. So there needs to be some measure of what my friend Rich and I call, "the degree of interconnectedness" of risks. **If we can understand how one risk is interconnected to the others, then it will help us to find solutions that will mitigate one or more of them simultaneously.** How about that?

In order to drive this home, I want to give you some examples. New technology has made it possible for light to be provided at the same brightness but with much less power expended. The incandescent bulbs consume a lot of power and excessive heat compared to new technologies. LED lights and CFL lights have been able to do the job for much less cost. This is the basic innovation. Now it is simply a matter of applying the innovation to the real world as a system.

This worked particularly well in my basement and my garage, although I don't recall seeing a noticeable change to my electric bill. There are so many other variables in the metric that it would be almost impossible for me to see the change, but I feel better knowing that I am being a good citizen and helping the environment.

Some people decided that we could improve upon the standard traffic light by putting several small LED lights to replace the incandescent bulbs. I imagine that they built several prototypes and got the specifications just about the same. They then invested in production and marketed the products to municipalities as a great investment to save electricity. Many municipalities bought into this concept and saved a lot of money in electricity by going "green."

Some that live in snowy climates probably got a big surprise after the first major snowfall. You see, the extra heat from the incandescent traffic lights melted the snow on the traffic lights so that drivers can see the signals in bad weather. The new LED traffic lights were fairly ineffective at meeting this "requirement." This created new challenges -- traffic mishaps and traffic delays. People can't see the lights any more. I call these **unintended consequences** of "improvements" to the system. One size does not fit all.

The new traffic lights worked exactly as designed, although when it was put into a specific, real-world scenario, it didn't meet the need, which was to provide safe travel 24/7 through the intersection (or something like that). You have to identify what it is that you need very carefully.

This is also an example of why you need good system engineers. Failure to have adequate system requirements can be disastrous. You can't just build it and hope that they will come either. It gets too easy to lose sight of the end state.

Here's another pitfall that often happens. Sometimes, we repurpose metrics for other uses inappropriately. Let's take standard school grades. It is used to measure learning progress at school. What happens when we use these same grades to determine placement in college? It is reasonable to think that good grades and success in college are highly correlated. But it also creates unintended consequences, like developing students who are afraid to fail.

Have a discussion with someone about the deeper impacts of important ideas. Draw a system model on a napkin, and have some fun with it! It will make you a better decision-maker and leader.

27

Dealing with Politics

" We are large enough to be grossly inefficient...and get away with it."—*anonymous coworker*

I am probably not the best person to write this chapter, because I am not a big fan of playing politics.

Whether you like it or not, there are likely to be some politics in play within any organization. The best organizations minimize this, but to say that it does not happen is just living in Fantasy Land with unicorns.

The 4 P's of a successful career are:
1. Performance
2. Potential
3. Politics
4. Luck

I know – luck does not begin with P, but that's why you will never forget it.

I knew a person who was trying at all costs to make himself look good at the expense of others. He was not willing to deal with the legitimate issues within his team since it would be seen as a weakness. He was quick to defend and find alternative reasons for the perceived failures.
- If he overcommitted, then the customer changed the deadlines.
- If he committed an ethical breach, there was outright denial. "That didn't happen, not on my watch."

- If there was incompetence, there was a lack of good requirements.

The sad reality is that the leader actually believed these things. In order to keep the deception going, he had to think and feel that way. If he could keep this façade up long enough, he would get promoted so that he can fix all of those other people who are "causing the problems."

My father taught me about the Peter Principle. The Peter Principle is a concept in management theory formulated by Laurence J. Peter in which the selection of a candidate for a position is based on the candidate's performance in their current role, rather than on abilities relevant to the intended role. Thus, employees only stop being promoted once they can no longer perform effectively, and "managers rise to the level of their incompetence." (Wikipedia)

In highly political organizations, there is a low level of trust, and some people are "acting." There has to be an agenda, and everyone seems to be up to something. It is usually easy to see the arrogance, superiority, resentment, and entitlement. It is harder to detect inward feelings of worry, stress, and fear (of being exposed for what I really am or fear of being judged). They are much easier to conceal if you have trained yourself well. At the end of the day, it's all an act.

Also, in a highly political organization, people are playing chess, making sure that they are three to five moves ahead of you. They play out the outcomes in their heads. They figure out how to win. Then they play the moves. That is exactly what it is too -- a game. They might tell a lie to see how someone will react. They might threaten to quit (even though they are not serious) to see if they can get their way. They might start a rumor just to see what happens. This is perverse business behavior.

What an exhausting way to work! You end up spending time doing all sorts of maneuvering, writing emails just so, and so forth.

I am not an advocate of weaseling your way to the top. But I don't want to be hard on people who've done it either. That's likely what they were being incentivized to do.

Let's turn this around for a second. Have I ever done that? Have I ever used people? Have I ever tried to ingratiate myself to the boss?

So how do you deal with politics?
1. Recognize and be sensitive to its existence.
2. Stay very clear on the proper objectives and results needed.
3. Do your best to achieve the right results in a way that helps other succeed too.
4. By doing so, you will succeed in cutting through to the truth and earning respect.
5. Recognize that it might come at a price, if you ruffle the feathers of the wrong person. That's where *luck* comes into play!

28

Developing Other Relevant Skills

"Don't let me do something stupid." - Anonymous boss
"Don't <u>make</u> me do something stupid." - Christian Hasselberg, subordinate

There are many skills that leaders need to be successful. I will list a few of them here:

You can't succeed without great management and process discipline...and great people.

Great people can be developed.

Develop your other business skills, such as Finance, Sales, Marketing, Human Resources, and Strategy. Go get an MBA.

It is often the leader who can write the best, figuring out what the award committee is looking for, that wins the awards. Therefore, don't neglect your writing skills.

Learn to give a good elevator speech.

Learn how to give a thank you speech.

Learn how to create passion around your ideas.

Make Measured Decisions. "Never let a crisis go to waste." Learn something from it. Not all problems are bad. It shows your value.

Learn to keep things simple for people. Understand the policy's intent vs. the letter of the law. Over-application of the rules is very wasteful and costly.

Don't ask a person to sacrifice if you are not willing to do the same.

Learn about Lean, Six Sigma and continuous improvement.

Stay good at Math. Practice.

Keep people motivated and focused on the mission.

Learn to write your own performance evaluation.

It is amazing how quickly people will see leadership inaction as a major morale killer.

Be patient with your leadership and help them.

Develop a strong network of friends and coworkers.

29

Continuous Improvement

"It can always be improved upon."

Continuous improvement is an umbrella term that is pretty self-explanatory. It is a way to rally a team around making an improvement to the way we do things.

I met a gentleman a few months ago, and we got to talking to about how well our company was at continuous improvement. Since I used to work for one of the competitors, I knew that we were at least five years behind and told him so.

I was really surprised at his reply: "If you don't like it here, go back!" He totally missed my point. There are several valuable lessons there. First, people are proud of their companies and can get defensive in the face of adverse facts and data. Second, we are trying to fix and improve where we are, not get defensive, bury our head in the sand and pretend that we are number one at everything. This can become an arrogance that is fatal. If you think you are #1 when you are not, that is a problem. Don't always buy into the hype.

There are several terms, such as Lean, Six Sigma and others. There are many models and methods, each that has its own purpose.

In general here are the 5 steps to make an improvement.
1. Visualize – what is the problem you are trying to solve? What would a future state look like?
2. Commit – Obtain the resources to complete the project and get a sponsor's approval.
3. Characterize – Describe the as-is and to-be state.
4. Improve – Make the improvements
5. Succeed – Measure success, document, and celebrate.

Then, repeat for the next project.

This simple model works for almost any improvement project. Here is a simple example:

1. Visualize. There are too many cell phones in the organization. We want the right number of phones.
2. Commit. The sponsor approves the project.
3. Characterize. Measure the usage rates and determine if people really need them.
4. Improve. Shut off the unneeded phones.
5. Succeed. Measure the savings over time and celebrate.

I really enjoyed the reading about how Alan Mulally worked with the team to turn Ford Motor Company around. (That is an excellent book, by the way.) As he did so, he found many inefficiencies. He said something like, "Thank God it wasn't Lean already...we'd be screwed."

I have a friend that thinks that people work because they have to in order to feed their families. In his opinion, that is the main driver. I think that is only partially true. Once the primary needs are met, I think that most people work because they want to fulfill themselves. In fact, they were meant to work. They want a challenge. They want to do something important. They want to be more successful. People are complex creatures. They want to challenged, and working on continuous improvement projects provides that fulfillment while also cutting costs for the organization. It is also very tangible and generally quick to see quantifiable results.

Generally, savings are categorized as cost savings or cost avoidance. You are either saving money right now, or you are avoiding costs in the future. Both have merit. Another thing to consider is who is benefitting from the improvement? Is your customer seeing this benefit in some way?

At one company that was training continuous improvement, they played a game called, "Win All You Can!" They broke the group into four teams and had them secretly choose a "blue ball" or "green ball." There were 10 rounds, including double bonus rounds. The scoring was a follows:

If the game host collected:
- four green balls: -1 point each.
- three green and one blue: the green teams get 1 point each and the team that submitted blue gets -3 points
- two green and two blue: +2 for green teams and -2 for blue teams
- one green and three blue: +3 for the green team and -1 each for the blue teams
- four blue balls: +1 point each

The leaders in the company were trying to get the bonus and win more than others, so there were all sorts of tactics going on to see who could get everyone else to play blue while they played green!

In this game, the only way that everyone wins is if everyone always plays blue, because only then does everyone WIN. That means that you have to think across the organization in order to achieve results. Continuous improvement that sub-optimizes in one area while hurting another area does not produce lasting improvement.

Mt friend Curtiss Witt recently wrote a book called "Gaming to Innovate, The Innovation Game" that makes coming up with innovative ideas fun and more engaging. It has a host of nuggets to help spawn new ideas. Make it fun for people!

Can you think of continuous improvement opportunities you could offer to do for your organization? If you do, you will become a valuable leader and connect with new people.

30

Giving Back

"I hope that my achievements in life shall be these - that I will have fought for what was right and fair, that I will have risked for that which mattered, and that I will have given help to those who were in need, that I will have left the earth a better place for what I've done and who I've been." – C. Hoppe

My friend Bob wrote an entire book on giving back, and I am going to devote a chapter to it as well.

I cannot express how fun it can be to serve others. It can be a lot of work, but it is also rewarding. Large or small, start where you are.

We need people who are willing to take their passions and give back to the community. There are many ways to do this. Go where your passions take you.

Speaking and teaching kids at local schools

Mentoring fellow employees

Teach Sunday school at a local church.

Help at a hospital

Performing work for a not for profit service

Picking up garbage along the road

Society needs you!

To lead is to serve. Who are you serving?

I enjoy doing construction, so I like to volunteer with Rebuilding Together, which is like Habitat for Humanity. We swarm a house with volunteers and fix up the place, usually in a day. Our last project was to fix a garage that had a tree fall through the roof. The garage was leaning almost 10 degrees. The experts told us to tear it down, but we had enough engineering skill to be dangerous, and we wanted to save it for the homeowner. It took us an extra day of planning, but we managed to repair the structure and put a new roof on it. We were so thrilled and honored to do it for her. It was hard work, but it was worth it!

Frantic Sidebar – Tour De Donut

I have been lucky to be the President of a local Bicycle club as well as Race Director of the Original Tour De Donut for the last five years. The Tour De Donut is a spoof on the Tour De France that takes place in Staunton, IL on the second Saturday in July. Bikers ride along a 34 mile course that has two donut stops. For every donut eaten, the rider gets a 5 minute time bonus. Yum! We are #29 in the top #35 most interesting rides in America.

We have attracted over 1,300 riders for the last three years and have donated over $50,000 for cycling-related causes and the local area. For more information about the world famous Tour De Donut, you can check out www.tourdedonut.org

Can one person make a difference in the face of significant challenges or dysfunction in organizations and in our society? The answer is absolutely yes. You may be swimming upstream. It also gets harder and harder to fight if people around you are not exhibiting the same values and leadership that you are. However, let me encourage you to stick to your values and always do the right thing. Don't be afraid of criticism; look for the truth in it, adjust, and throw the rest away.

I wish you great success on your leadership journey!

Feel free to drop me a line and let me know what you think of this book at christian@franticleader.com.

I look forward to hearing from you. If you or your organization need to get to that next level, I would be honored to help.

Appendix
A

Books I Recommend

People often ask me what some good books to read are. There are a lot of books out there and only so much time. Here are a few recommendations that I really enjoyed:

Leadership and Self-Deception by the Arbinger Institute, 5 stars
The Anatomy of Peace by the Arbinger Institute, 5 stars
The **Outward Mindset**, by the Arbinger Institute, 5 stars
American Icon, Alan Mulally and the fight to save Ford Motor Company by Bryce G. Hoffman, 5 stars
Steve Jobs by Walter Isaacson, 5 stars
Thinking in Systems by Donella Meadows, 5 stars
Getting to Yes: **Negotiating Agreement without Giving In** by Roger Fisher, William L. Ury and Bruce Patton, 5 stars
How to Measure Anything, by Douglas Hubbard, 5 stars
Work Rules, by Laszlo Bock, 5 stars
Moneyball by Michael Lewis, 4 stars
The Heart of Change by John Kotter, 4 stars
Your Brain on a Bike by John Brent Pye, 4 stars
The Turnaround Kid, by Steve Miller, 4 stars
The Rickover Effect: The Inside Story of How Adm. Hyman Rickover Built the Nuclear Navy by Theodore Rockwell, 4 stars
Eleven Rings, The Soul of Success by Phil Jackson, 4 stars
Wooden by Coach Wooden, 4 stars
Leading with the Heart: Coach K's Successful Strategies for Basketball, Business, and Life by Mike Krzyzewski, Donald T. Phillips and Grant Hill, 4 stars

You will notice that some of the prevailing leadership guru books are not on my list. It is likely that I have read many of them, and feel free to do so if you like. I have found that some of them were not as helpful for me, so I do not recommend them on the first tier.

INDEX

ABOUT THE AUTHOR

Christian Hasselberg was born in upstate New York and grew up in Meriden, Connecticut. His parents taught by example that you never fail if you keep getting back up.

As the second of four children, Hasselberg learned early in life to become self-reliant. He spent a lot of time with his best friend and entrepreneur James Williams and Jamie's family working odd jobs at the school of hard knocks.

Christian graduated high school 3rd in his class and went to the University of Idaho on a Naval Reserve Officer Training Corps scholarship to earn a degree in Computer Science. He then moved to Virginia to attend Naval Intelligence School and serve about the USS DWIGHT D EISENHOWER (CVN-69) aircraft carrier. He earned a Master in Information Technology from Webster University.

After leaving the Navy, Christian went to work in the civilian sector in Tucson, Arizona, where he also earned a Master's in Business Administration at the University of Arizona. He returned to the St. Louis, Missouri area in 2006 and resides there. He has been in leadership roles for 25-30 years. He is also licensed to sell real estate.

He lives with his first wife Michelle and their three children, Nathan, Victoria, and Karsten. He enjoys cycling, fishing, reading, learning, leadership, and much more. He is the President of a local bicycle club, a local leadership association and is the race director for the Original Tour De Donut, ranked #29 most interesting bike races in America.

For information visit: **www.outoftheboxbooks.com**. You can contact the author via e-mail at: **christian@franticleader.com**

www.ingramcontent.com/pod-product-compliance
Lightning Source LLC
Chambersburg PA
CBHW020201200326
41521CB00005BA/210